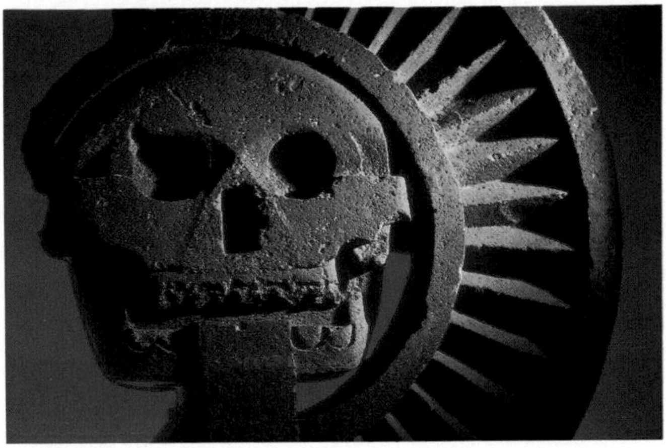

THE MIGHTY
AZTECS

By Gene S. Stuart
Photographs by Mark Godfrey
Paintings by Louis S. Glanzman

Prepared by the Special Publications Division
National Geographic Society, Washington, D.C.

THE MIGHTY AZTECS

By Gene S. Stuart

Photographs by Mark Godfrey

Paintings by Louis S. Glanzman

Dr. Henry B. Nicholson, *Consultant, Professor of Anthropology, University of California, Los Angeles*

Published by
  The National Geographic Society
  Gilbert M. Grosvenor, *President*
  Melvin M. Payne, *Chairman of the Board*
  Owen R. Anderson, *Executive Vice President*
  Robert L. Breeden, *Vice President, Publications and Educational Media*

Prepared by
  The Special Publications Division
  Donald J. Crump, *Editor*
  Philip B. Silcott, *Associate Editor*
  William L. Allen, William R. Gray, *Senior Editors*

Staff for this Book
  Mary Ann Harrell, *Managing Editor*
  Thomas B. Powell III, *Picture Editor*
  Ursula P. Vosseler, *Art Director*
  Sallie M. Greenwood, *Senior Researcher;* Monique F. Einhorn, Karen M. Kostyal, *Researchers*

Illustrations and Design
  Lynette R. Ruschak, *Designer*
  Mark Seidler, *Artist for Chapter Emblems*
  John D. Garst, Jr., Virginia L. Baza, Margaret Deane Gray, Gary M. Johnson, Susan M. Johnston, Mark Seidler, *Map Research, Design, and Production*
  Louis De La Haba, Toni Eugene, Judith A. Folkenberg, Karen M. Kostyal, Thomas O'Neill, Kathleen F. Teter, Suzanne Venino, *Picture Legend Writers*

Engraving, Printing and Product Manufacture
  Robert W. Messer, *Manager*
  George V. White, *Production Manager*
  Richard A. McClure, *Production Project Manager*
  Mark R. Dunlevy, Raja D. Murshed, Christine A. Roberts, David V. Showers, Gregory Storer, *Assistant Production Managers*
  Mary A. Bennett, Kate Donohue, *Production Staff Assistants*
Debra A. Antonini, Nancy F. Berry, Pamela A. Black, Barbara Bricks, Nettie Burke, Jane H. Buxton, Mary Elizabeth Davis, Claire M. Doig, Rosamund Garner, Victoria D. Garrett, Nancy J. Harvey, Joan Hurst, Suzanne J. Jacobson, Artemis S. Lampathakis, Virginia A. McCoy, Merrick P. Murdock, Cleo Petroff, Victoria I. Piscopo, Tammy Presley, Jane F. Ray, Carol A. Rocheleau, Katheryn M. Slocum, Jenny Takacs, *Staff Assistants*
George I. Burneston, III, *Index*

Library of Congress CIP Data: page 198.

Preceding pages: Cloud wreathes the peak of Chalcatzingo, in eastern Morelos. Page 1: A stone disk from Teotihuacan may foreshadow Aztec portrayals of a Lord of the Dead, Mictlantecutli, as a skull with lolling tongue and pleated paper crown. Hardcover: Redrawn from the work of an Indian artist, the eagle on a prickly pear cactus recalls the portent that marked the site of the Aztec capital, Tenochtitlan.

CONTENTS

DAVID HISER

Preparing a staple known for centuries, women of Texcoco pat cornmeal dough into tortillas. They ground the maize on slabs called metates *with stone rollers,* manos. *The Aztecs ate tortillas daily; hands patting dough appear on the glyph, or symbol, of the ancient city Tlaxcala.*

AUTUMN, 1519

The land comes gently to the tropic sea at Veracruz, slipping beneath waves that often mirror the sky. Toward the horizon brilliant dark blue joins a like blue as one, or somber clouds meld with a churning gray sea until the horizon is undefinable. At those times what the eye can see becomes an encircling world apart, sealed away from other realities like the vision in a sorcerer's mirror. Men far from home, on small Spanish ships in a peaceful bay in the spring of 1519, may have noted such impressions before turning to face the land and the kaleidoscope of changes there that come with shifting light.

The shore was awesome: shimmering beaches, marshland of a mysterious mood, gigantic sand dunes that shifted with the whim of wind, a tangle of tropical forest beyond. The familiar world closed behind them. Their leader, Hernán Cortés, destroyed his ships so there could be no question of turning back. He would lead them inland to the heart of this new world.

A constant, looming above, was a range of forbidding mountains. And above all, a snow-ringed volcano with a superbly graduated cone soared so high the clouds rarely parted to expose its glistening splendor. That peak is Orizaba. To the Spanish adventurers, it and the mountains surrounding it became landmarks on a route of conquest. The ranges bordered realms that Cortés would claim for Spain and souls that priests would save for God.

To the Indian peoples, mountains were sacred—places of miracle. Their peaks, caves, and clear-running mountain streams were lairs of capricious gods who demanded supplication and offerings. Their bounty was often twofold. With the blessings of rain came devastating thunderbolts; with sacred free-flowing springs came precipitous dark ravines.

In a letter to the Emperor Charles V, King of Spain, Cortés noted his army's difficulties as they struggled along beyond their first mountain pass: "we were assailed by a whirlwind of hailstones and rain in which I thought many were like to die of cold: and certain Indians from Cuba who were scantily clothed did indeed thus perish." High in another pass he found "a small tower almost like a roadside chapel, in which certain idols were kept. . . ."

Spaniards toppled many of these sacred images to replace them with the Christian cross. Some represented local gods; others, Aztec deities ensconced in temples by the powerful Aztec Empire as it spread, conquering gods and humans alike. Warriors of these Indian kingdoms joined Cortés in his march on the capital of the hated Aztecs, eager to rid themselves of a cruel and demanding supremacy.

In their own embattled past, in defeat and in victory, the Aztecs had developed a haunting sense of the uncertainty of all power, all mortal things, even all gods. Four "suns" or ages, they said, had perished in universal ruin. They lived in the fifth sun, itself inevitably doomed.

Now spies and emissaries reported the Spaniards' every move to their sacred lord, Moctezuma II, in his capital at Tenochtitlan. Terrified by omens, he spent long hours consulting his advisers, performing sacred rites, doing penance, or sitting alone pondering the possibility that this already-legendary being, bearded and clad in metal, could be the god Quetzalcoatl, returning to claim his domain.

Cortés advanced with the confidence of a conqueror. As he moved westward to the last great mountain barriers, the volcanoes Popocatepetl and Iztaccihuatl, Moctezuma again sent emissaries eastward. A high pass between the volcanoes separated the two parties. By now, winter was approaching. November on the high slopes can bring freezing storms, winds whirling volcanic sand so sharp it seems to attack like hundreds of obsidian knives. Yet Cortés chose to ascend.

Popocatepetl, an active volcano, threatened disaster. From it, the Spanish leader wrote, "both by day and night a great volume of smoke often comes forth and rises up into the clouds as straight as a staff. . . ." Even in the violent wind that continually swept over the heights, this pillar of smoke did not bend. Cortés sent men "to find out the secret of the smoke, where and how it arose." They were near the top when smoke gushed up, "with such noise and violence that the whole mountain seemed like to fall down. . . ."

With the uncanny shuddering movement of earthquakes, said the Aztecs, the Fifth Sun would die.

*U*pward the armored invaders climbed, past the great pines cherished by the Aztecs, leading fierce mastiffs and guarding their few precious horses in the thin cold air. From the other side of the volcano, Moctezuma's emissaries hurried forward, splendid in their capes trimmed with bright tropical feathers, their jewels of jade and turquoise and gold. As the Spaniards ascended, thousands of Indian allies followed, clad in quilted cotton armor. The army, ready with Spanish steel swords and Indian stone-tipped darts, approached the pass. One of Cortés's soldiers, Bernal Díaz, recalled, "As we came to the top it began to snow, and the snow caked on the ground." At that moment the Spaniards stood with cross and sword between two mountains profoundly sacred to the Aztecs.

By nightfall they were descending; they bivouacked in shelters built for the use of traveling Aztec traders. "Then we posted our sentries, organized our patrols, manned some listening-posts, and sent out scouting parties."

In the gray light of dawn, Aztecs and Spaniards prayed to their respective gods and prepared for one of history's most awesome confrontations.

Opposite: Hernán Cortés, bound for the capital of the Aztec Empire, meets envoys of the Tlaxcalans, the people who became his key allies. His interpreter Doña Marina points to him as the envoys offer food. A Tlaxcalan artist painted this for an account of the mighty Aztecs' defeat.

Rainwater mirrors the Pyramid of the Moon at the great site called Teotihuacan, or Place of the Gods, by marveling Aztecs, who knew it only as an awe-inspiring ruin from the mythic past.

November wind whips snow from the volcano Popocatepetl above the Pass of Cortés—on the conquistadores' invasion route.

Cortés surveys the island city Tenochtitlan, capital of the Aztec Empire. Aztec lords escort him. The artist sets his party on high ground to portray the skyline, now often veiled in smog; the lakes of the Valley of Mexico, now largely drained or dried or filled in; and the city, destroyed in the Spanish conquest.

Moon of the Aztecs: A Broken Glory

Relic of ancient glory, this carving of the goddess Coyolxauhqui lies where the lords of Tenochtitlan placed it: before their greatest temple, El Templo Mayor *in the Spanish tongue. In 1978, a ditchdigger discovered the stone; experts from* INAH, *Mexico's National Institute of Anthropology and History, have exposed and cleaned it. This find prompted fulfillment of plans to excavate the temple, with results that delight citizens of Mexico, archaeologists everywhere, and anyone intrigued by the dramatic Aztec past. Weight and stress had cracked the stone, which honors the first victory of a tribal god. The folk who called themselves the Mexica told this myth: By a miracle the Earth Mother conceived her last son, Huitzilopochtli. His brothers, urged on by their sister Coyolxauhqui, decided to kill her. Born a warrior and fully armed, Huitzilopochtli saved his mother; he beheaded and dismembered Coyolxauhqui. Priests of the Aztec Empire rolled the bodies of sacrificial victims down the steps of his temple to fall beside this monument. Appalled by such rites, the Spaniards fought to destroy the power of Tenochtitlan—and the faith that had inspired it from the beginning.*

DAVID HISER

THE SETTING

"The remains of what they made and left behind are still there and can be seen, among them.... the structures of stone and earth...."

At times I walked above the trees. Always, I stood beneath the snow. I was earthbound, yet roaming higher, separated from the world far below by a thick layer of clouds as I walked through the Pass of Cortés and wandered along the slopes of the two volcanoes, Popocatepetl and Iztaccihuatl. By the calendar it was November 4, within hours of the time the Spanish conqueror and his armies passed through—if one ignores an additional 461 years. That morning I chose to forget the years and remember the hours.

I was seeking something—a fleeting impression—of what the Spaniards had experienced centuries before. For warmth I wore two sweaters, together probably heavier than the garb of ill-prepared invaders newly arrived from the tropics. At just over 12,000 feet, the pass is a broad, windy

Preceding pages: Morning's blaze behind a pyramid at Teotihuacan evokes creation of the sun in Aztec mythology. To the southwest in the Valley of Mexico, the Aztecs rose to power in the 15th century.

PRECEDING PAGES: ALBERT MOLDVAY
EMBLEM, ABOVE: THE GOD TLALOC

meadow lying mostly above the timberline and below the autumn snow line. A storm the night before had wrapped Popo in a new covering of white, dusted Izta lightly, but left the pass clear. It had swept the thin air so clear and cold that each sudden gasp between normal breaths had to be held in the mouth like a sliver of ice before being swallowed. As the veteran Bernal Díaz del Castillo recalled in matter-of-fact understatement, "the cold was intense." Soon my fingers seemed disjointed when I reached up to test my icicle nose.

I had hoped for the fresh snow Díaz had described, but instead found thick hummocks of long grass blowing free in the wind. Stumbling seemed the normal mode of travel. With snow, the footing for horses must have been difficult. From the pass I went far down into the dark, foreboding forest along a narrow dirt road that may well follow the route of the armies. On Popo I walked to within yards of the snow line, plodding through black volcanic sand to pause at the edge of a ravine as wind whirled a cloud from deep inside like steam from a boiling fissure. I heard birds twitter in the highest range of the tall pines below. On Izta I watched a bumblebee drone its way among pink thistles and small blue blossoms. Finally, I, too, felt the sudden icy sting of swirling snowflakes against my face. And always the sound of the timeless wind like a wide, flowing river was with me across the centuries. In climbing Izta, I found even more than I had hoped for. In a sense I saw the mountain as people

18

knew it long before the Spaniards arrived.

Across a wide ravine, in a dark ridge of lava, I suddenly saw the squared entrance to a black cave. I gazed at it for a long time, remembering that Aztecs held mountains and caves sacred, as did peoples already ancient when Aztecs came upon the scene. A Spanish priest, Fray Diego Durán, wrote of the Aztec compulsion to "burn incense in dark and fearsome caves where the idols were kept, where special ceremonies were conducted. . . ." One cave on Izta had sheltered such deities: among them a carving of Iztaccihuatl, White Lady, the mountain itself as a goddess, as well as one of Tlaloc, the god of rain, storms, and caves. I wondered if this was that sacred Aztec cave.

The Aztecs had adopted Tlaloc and other ancient deities into their own pantheon. Always self-consciously aware that they were latecomers in the dramatic history of the Valley of Mexico, they could not know how long that story actually is.

It may stretch back more than thirty thousand years to the Ice Age mammals. Mammoths, camels, and horses foraged on the muddy lakeshores and stalwart hunters preyed upon them. Yet even before many of the large animals became extinct these astute people were stalking or trapping smaller game, gathering wild foods.

About 5000 B.C. a slow change began. The rudiments of agriculture came into the valley, and people settled into small villages. Hunting and gathering continued; but pumpkins, beans, chili peppers, amaranth, and eventually maize became the staples of an agrarian diet. By 1500 B.C. farming was the life pattern in most of Mesoamerica. (This is the cultural area from present-day central Mexico to a southern border that varied through time; it included modern Honduras, Belize, Guatemala, and El Salvador.)

New skills heightened the quality of life: weaving, pottery-making, shaping stones to grind grain. Then change accelerated when Mesoamerica's first great civilization, the Olmec, rose from the sultry coastal lowlands of western Tabasco and southern Veracruz.

There broad rivers teem with fauna for the taking; rainfall is ample, the best land extremely fertile. Dynastic rulers appeared, apparently combining the roles of chieftain and priest or god, commanding workers in esoteric new labor.

Beginning about 1200 B.C. these mysterious Olmec people built a series of great centers to which people from outlying villages probably journeyed on religious pilgrimages. Earthen mounds surrounded courtyards. Temples with thatched roofs topped large earthen pyramids. One site, San Lorenzo, occupied an immense artificial plateau. Stone conduits filled pools possibly used for ceremonial bathing. At La Venta a huge mound of earth and clay

Objects of Awe

Antiquities to the Aztecs, these artifacts come from much more ancient cultures. The Olmecs, Mesoamerica's first great civilization, fashioned the mask three millennia ago; long afterward, the Aztecs revered it at their greatest temple. The "pretty lady" figurine from a site called Tlatilco suggests the favor of fertility and the philosophy of duality. Cosmic opposites pit the wet against the dry, day against night, life against death—and haunt Mesoamerica from Olmec to Aztec times.

resembled a volcano. Nearby, mosaic pavements formed jaguar masks.

Olmec sculptors carved Mesoamerica's first large monuments, and traveled more than forty miles into the mountains for basalt chunks as heavy as twenty tons. As many as a thousand workers dragged these with ropes and floated them homeward on rafts to be finished as altars or portrait heads for the great centers. At intervals, it seems, these great monuments were defaced and buried and new ones prepared.

Smaller, unmarred figurines of fine clays and rare stones show ball players, fat petulant babies and snarling jaguars. Many portray a sacred human-jaguar figure with fangs and a turned-down mouth—possibly a rain god and precursor of many later rain deities including Tlaloc. Intellectual developments were one with religious and artistic accomplishments. Olmec sages may have developed a calendar; builders apparently oriented sites to the movement of celestial bodies.

Long before the Olmecs reached their zenith, their ideas and influence spread. Networks of trade—or far-flung colonies— introduced them to most of Mesoamerica, and with them went the seeds of civilization. The walls of caves in Guerrero bear Olmec paintings; at Chalcatzingo a dignitary—or deity—sculpted in stone sits enthroned on a mountainside and gazes across a wide valley toward Popo. Finely worked jades unearthed in El Salvador and Costa Rica had been valued enough to be carried hundreds of miles.

Veins of obsidian thread volcanic mountains and link cultures in northern Mesoamerica. Archaeologist Manfred Sasso Guardia, right, examines debris in a mine near Teotihuacan, where rich deposits supplied the city that dominated the region from 100 B.C. to A.D. 750. Ancient peoples used this natural glass for sharp-edged tools, weapons, and items of trade.

But with Olmec splendor archaeologists have also found the somber—human remains show unmistakable signs of cannibalism down the years. And about 900 B.C. building ceased at San Lorenzo. La Venta carried on longer—a century, or several— and it, too, fell. People who came later to loot it must have had some sense of its significance—they left offerings in the ruins.

Long before the downfall of the coastal centers, it seems, something of Olmec ritual became known in the Valley of Mexico, largest of the high basins of the central Mexican plateau. Because it lacked drainage to the sea, its streams fed a chain of shallow lakes, and farming peoples were settled in flourishing villages on the shores of Lake Texcoco. The highlanders had already developed distinctive traits of their own. The site called Tlatilco, once a riverside community near the lake, now lies beneath brickyards in Mexico City. Its graves held some relics of Olmec style and many which are utterly different—notably the tiny clay figurines.

A few of the figurines depict men, but most portray women with stubby arms and large, rounded thighs. Many wear a short low-slung flounce of a skirt, or saucy bloomers. Some wear nothing more than a necklace. Most have for adornment only a grandiose coiffure. One critic thinks the "figurines reflect the happiness, ingenuity, enchantment and positiveness of a cult completely saturated with symbolism of fertility, the earth and growth."

While these "pretty ladies" charm, they can also confound, for many have puzzled experts for years: statuettes of a surrealistic quality, with two heads or one head and multiple sets of features. They may well personify duality.

Other villagers of the valley were producing small figurines, about 400 B.C., when the people of Cuicuilco, on the southwestern shore of Lake Texcoco, took

religion a step further. They built a center dominated by a large temple platform, with double altars at the top. Such buildings meant laborers to construct them, and leaders with power to command. As Cuicuilco and other centers developed, people no longer interred the were-jaguar images of the Olmec. Archaeologist Muriel Porter Weaver suggests, "Perhaps they felt less apprehensive of the jaguar than of . . . the Old Fire God, who controlled the restless volcanoes close by."

The volcano called Xitle, it seems,

Abode of the Gods

Silence shrouds the city erected to the glory of the gods at Teotihuacan. Today only the pyramids, the long avenue, and the vast remains of temples and districts attest to the religious fervor that mobilized this first urban culture into such massive construction and artistic endeavor. Five centuries after the city's fall, the Aztecs marveled at the immensity of the pyramids and quickly ascribed these wonders to deities, adapting myths to link the creation of their era with that of the buildings. Frequently visited by the Aztecs, Teotihuacan ranked as a ritual and pilgrimage center even in ruins.

checked the ascendancy of Cuicuilco. One flow of lava covered productive fields; a later eruption buried the center itself. Long afterward I stood in the partially excavated ruins in the southern part of Mexico City, glanced at the hulking mountain, and shivered on a balmy summer afternoon.

Beyond the reach of Xitle, on the edge of the basin some 35 miles northeast, another center took shape: a village that matured into a metropolis and dominated much of Mesoamerica for 750 years—mighty Teotihuacan. It stood unique in the New World, conceived with majesty and executed on such a grand scale its magnificence was never matched again.

Teotihuacan—the name seems to mean Place of the Gods, or Place Where Men Become Gods. Aztecs called it this when they visited the ruined city centuries after its collapse, enshrined it in their own myths, and explained the structures along its most imposing avenue as tombs of ancient kings who had become gods. That avenue they called Way of the Dead; they called the enormous structures that loom

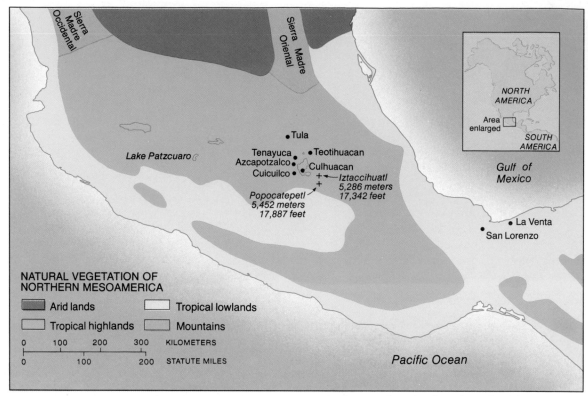

Northern Mesoamerica encompasses lush coastal lowlands, where the Olmec culture took form and flourished, and resource-rich highlands, eventual domain of the Aztecs.

above it the Pyramids of the Sun and Moon. Indeed, these celestial bodies were born there, Aztecs said, after the sun had been destroyed four times. Two gods had sacrificed themselves by leaping into a fire, to become the sun and moon we see today.

Evidently planned as it grew, the city spread in four major quadrants defined by two broad avenues that led to the center. Streets and alleyways divided the quadrants into smaller squares, each separated into apartment compounds with entrances and patios arranged to give each household privacy. People from faraway Oaxaca, merchants, potters, and stoneworkers settled into distinct neighborhoods. Glassy scraps in profusion mark the areas where craftsmen shaped obsidian into tools and weapons for local use and export.

Residences stood densely packed in the northwest area of the eight-square-mile city. Arable land spread to the east and to the southwest, producing food for the masses.

By recent estimates, as many as 200,000 people may have lived in Teotihuacan at its peak, about A.D. 600. The total must have risen by the thousand when pilgrims arrived from afar. They probably lingered to transact business, collect news, spread gossip, and marvel at a swarming cosmopolitan life, for this was the spiritual, political, and economic hub of Mesoamerica.

The city elite who administered matters of state had elegant palaces, where rooms bright with murals opened onto sunny patios. Temples still bear representations of powerful gods; a goggle-eyed and fanged deity, and a plumed serpent,

Heads of a feathered snake and masks of a goggle-eyed god alternate on a temple at Teotihuacan. To the Aztecs such forms evoked two mighty deities: Tlaloc, the rain god, and Quetzalcoatl, or Plumed Serpent, who may reveal himself as wind.

Skins for clothing, bows and arrows, and bundled-up possessions characterize Chichimec bands wandering the desolate north. Moving southward over hundreds of years, these peoples blended with civilized folk around the Valley of Mexico. One group, known as Aztecs, stood out as crude and combative.

suggest Tlaloc and Quetzalcoatl, held in awe centuries later by the Aztecs. In all probability religion ranked with trade as a major factor in the rise of Teotihuacan.

An astounding discovery made in 1971 has strengthened this theory. Excavation at the Pyramid of the Sun revealed steps to a cave 110 yards long. Its ceilings had been lowered at intervals, says archaeologist René Millon, so anyone entering would have to crouch or kneel; charcoal in abundance suggested rituals of fire, stone channels implied rituals of water. The passage ended in a cloverleaf of chambers beneath the pyramid, near its center.

Archaeologist Doris Heyden sees many possibilities for use of the grotto, holiest of places. Perhaps it was sacred because caves were considered the womb of earth, and many myths of origin tell of ancestors emerging from caves. It may have been a place of secret investiture ceremonies for rulers and priests; of sacred rites to earth and water deities, of human sacrifice to please them; of death rites for the elite; of divination or visits to an oracle to ask the fate of the realm at the hands of capricious gods. Such caves of mystical power still draw thousands of devoted pilgrims in modern-day Mexico.

Through the years I have made many pilgrimages of my own to Teotihuacan. Recently I spent several days revisiting it once again. On a late afternoon I climbed worn stone stairways to the slow plaintive sounds of clay flutes in the shape of ancient gods, played by souvenir hawkers along the Way of the Dead. In the fading light pyramids echoed the shapes of nearby mountains. A cold wind stirred as a distant storm swept the valley with sheaths of rain and bolts of lightning. I thought of the Aztecs and their belief that Quetzalcoatl as the wind god sweeps the road and cleanses it for Tlaloc to follow with fertilizing rain. At sunset thunder still rumbled.

I rose before dawn hoping to see the sun rise in the place where it came to life—carried aloft, it was believed, from the underworld to its zenith by Aztec warriors killed in battle, and sustained by the blood of human sacrifice. Raindrops spread circles in puddles of water in front of my door. Outside it was as dark as if the sun had never been created.

By noon the storm was breaking. At that hour, legend says, Aztec women who died in childbirth took the sun to speed it on its downward journey toward sunset, as low-angled beams sparked each green blade with golden fire, lit bamboo stalks from within with an amber glow, and touched a scarlet flower to flame. Gray clouds blended with the horizon as the sun slipped into the underworld. Only a pallid light remained.

Such splendors of color enriched the deeply religious art of Teotihuacan. Gods, priests, and mythical animals were depicted in fine ceramics, carved in stone, painted on temple walls. In one mural, people frolic among beasts, birds, and butterflies beneath shade trees near a mountain of water—a tropical paradise.

But late in the city's history its art reveals a change: a new imagery of war. Priests and deities appear wearing helmets, carrying shields and weapons. In this, René Millon sees evidence of a militarism which "may be both a symptom of difficulty and a cause of it." Trouble at home might stem from wars elsewhere. The state had far-flung interests to protect—even among the Maya, far to the southeast—and barbarians were at another border.

Overleaf: Warrior columns, carved in basalt, bear witness to militarism in Quetzalcoatl's temple at Tula, a capital from about 900 to 1200. Aztecs glorified ties to the imperialistic Toltecs and to Chichimec ancestors to embellish their past and to emphasize their might.

City of Warriors

*Once showcase and stronghold, the city of
Tula stands now stripped of its splendor.
Legend credits it with stunning temples,
grand ball courts, and a colorful plaza, but
its shoddily built structures and half-
remembered history hint that this state
devoted its energy to far-flung wars. The
so-called Chac Mool, reclining in stone,
perhaps conveyed messages to Toltec gods;
its secrets remain today among the
mysteries of Tula.*

North and west of the Valley of Mexico
lay the arid zone called the Gran Chichi-
meca, home of scattered roving bands, and
along its margins lived peoples more or less
acquainted with civilization. The name
Chichimec, People of the Place of the Dog,
refers to all of them; and any change in climate would affect them all.

Local droughts may have brought
famine to the valley, increasing social ten-
sions in the city. For whatever reason, destruction came upon it, apparently without

bloodshed. Fires, deliberately set, ravaged
the great buildings of the center. René
Millon thinks the Aztec myth of the sun's
creation may derive from the city's own
faith. "If so," he writes, "what was created
in fire was destroyed by fire, abruptly, vio-
lently, cataclysmically." He compares this
to ritual destruction at other sites, as in
Olmec times.

Had the gods demanded too much
and given too little in return? Whatever the
answer, Teotihuacan declined. By A.D. 750

its political importance was done. Most of its people were living in scattered settlements nearby. Yet an aura of the sacred remained. Along the Way of the Dead archaeologists find remnants of small structures that may date from Aztec times.

Mesoamericans kept the old gods alive, but the new conspicuous militarism would inspire each succeeding power until the Spanish conquest. Less than fifty miles away, near the line where scanty rainfall precludes agriculture, the people called Toltec rose to rule the highlands from their capital, Tula. If Teotihuacan gave gods to the Aztecs it was the Toltecs who gave them heroes. Quetzalcoatl survived to reappear personified in Tula.

His story, like all Toltec history as the Aztecs told it to the Spaniards, lives in myths based on solid facts. Even the myths disagree, but most scholars think Toltec-Chichimec people from the northwest joined people already living in the central plateau to become empire builders. Their leader Mixcoatl, Cloud Serpent, settled in the Valley of Mexico and began conquering his neighbors. His glory was brief, however, for he was assassinated before his son was born. This son established Tula and became a high priest and reformer, the Quetzalcoatl of legend.

The Aztecs recalled the Toltecs as masters of wisdom, skilled artists and craftsmen. The great Quetzalcoatl presented them with all knowledge. He endowed agriculture with miraculous abundance—the squashes were immense, amaranth bushes were tall as trees, men could hardly get their arms around ears of corn. "In very many places there was chocolate," as Aztecs told a Franciscan priest, Fray Bernardino de Sahagún. Raw cotton needed no dyes: "bright red, yellow, rose colored, violet, green, azure, verdigris color, whitish, brown, shadowy, rose red, and coyote colored. . . . so they grew. . . ."

To live in Tula was to dwell in bliss. The Toltecs had "great riches, great wealth. . . . there was never famine. . . .

"And also, Quetzalcoatl did penance. He drew blood from the calves of his legs; he stained thorns with the blood. . . . And the priests modeled their lives on Quetzalcoatl's way of life. By means of it they established the laws of Tula. Thus the customs were established here. . . ."

It was said that Quetzalcoatl built palaces of fine green stone, gold, turquoise, coral, shells, and precious feathers. Loathing human sacrifice, the gentle priest pleased his benevolent god with offerings of snakes, jade, and butterflies.

Yet his story takes an ominous turn. His rival Tezcatlipoca, or Smoking Mirror, was Lord of the Night and patron of wizards and evil-doers. This all-powerful god demanded warfare and human sacrifice. Many scholars see this rivalry as an instance of the duality found so often in Mesoamerican religion. "The two deities are at war," wrote Mexican archaeologist Alfonso Caso, "and their struggles are the history of the Universe."

Followers of Tezcatlipoca tricked Quetzalcoatl into drunkenness and humiliation. Disgraced, he left Tula with his followers, traveling through the Valley of Mexico to the Gulf. There, one story says, he set fire to himself and rose into the sky to become Venus, the Morning and Evening Star. Another account says he sailed eastward, promising to return in the year One Reed, the anniversary of his birth, to rule his people once more.

Subsequent Toltec lords defended the empire from nomadic Chichimecs attacking from the north. Huemac, the last ruler, could not protect Tula from the final onslaught—when the Aztecs themselves may have been among the marauders. The city was burned, and most of the Toltecs fled. Some followed Huemac to Chapultepec, a promontory on the shore of Lake Texcoco, where the despondent old emperor committed suicide.

What of this tale is truth? In all likelihood there was a man called Quetzalcoatl who embraced the religion of his namesake god. He became such a hero that priests or rulers took his name, just as Aztec priests would assume it as a title. Certainly there was a Toltec state that controlled the highlands; and while it flourished, Toltec invaders conquered the Maya city of Chichen Itza, in Yucatan, and built a new capital grander than their old one.

The principal ruins at Tula today hardly evoke the superb city of Aztec legend. They occupy the top of a ridge above a river about fifty miles north of Mexico City, a spot easily defended. I found the sun bright, the wind cold, and Tula deserted except for two or three tourists wandering the temples and palaces and an old woman patiently coaxing a herd of sheep and goats across the grassy plaza. I was surrounded by militarism: stone warriors in feather headdresses and butterfly-shaped breastplates standing more than 15 feet tall; soldiers in war regalia carved in relief; a frieze of chieftains ready for battle.

Religion is here also. Eagles, jaguars, and feathered serpents decorate crumbling buildings. The mysterious reclining figures called Chac Mools stare vacantly at one another across a wide roofless palace where Quetzalcoatl may have sat in council. A carved column portrays a bearded personage with an elaborate headdress and a name sign that may mean Feathered Serpent. Glyphs represent Venus in his honor. But it was near the end of my visit that the city of Quetzalcoatl came alive for me. On a rough stone altar at my feet, a golden butterfly tinged with black lit and pulsed its delicate wings in the sunlight.

I saw nothing of Tezcatlipoca. It is as if the dreaded god of darkness were never here. After Tula fell, chaos reigned in central Mexico, but small independent city-

Robust sculpture found at Tula belies the superlative artistic and intellectual refinement later ascribed to the Toltecs. The warrior in quilted armor, who once supported an altar, embodies the mingling of warfare and religion that marked Tula and its successors. The Aztecs plotted and fought their way to mastery among city-states vying for power after Tula fell.

states developed on the shores of Lake Texcoco. One, Culhuacan, carried on Toltec traditions. Others, like Texcoco, were settled by Chichimecs from the north.

Another tribe of poor wandering Chichimecs—the tribe we know today as Aztecs—were on the move, led by their own god of war, Huitzilopochtli. What miserable people would not follow a god, however demanding, who promised: "we shall proceed to establish ourselves and settle down, and we shall conquer all peoples of the universe; and I tell you in all truth that I will make you lords and kings of all that is in the world. . . ."

THE WANDERERS

"They went along shooting their arrows; they had no houses, they had no lands, they had no woven capes as clothing...."

It must have changed in the telling from generation to generation. But the story was kept alive and repeated time and again. Fathers reminded sons; grandmothers thrilled wide-eyed youngsters huddled by the fire. Youths in school recited the old tales to exacting teachers who consulted painted books. Their history could not be forgotten.

The Aztecs came from obscurity, lifting themselves from misery to might, surviving calamitous misfortunes, enduring the most extreme hardships to prevail in the worst of times against their enemies. Aztecs took pride in their history even if no one envied them their past.

Preceding pages: Island town in a placid lake—so the Aztecs described the legendary home Aztlan, Place of Herons, from which they took their name. Experts debate its location, even its existence. Lake Patzcuaro, where a patriot's statue now crowns the isle Janitzio, fits the ancient account—and may have inspired it.

EMBLEM, ABOVE: THE GOD HUITZILOPOCHTLI

That began in a mysterious place sometimes remembered as Godland or The Place of Origin, but also described to Spanish priests as Aztlan, Place of Herons. It lay somewhere to the northwest where from an island in a lake men went out to fish from boats.

Of ultimate origins Fray Diego Durán wrote: "Some say that the Indians were born of springs of water; others say that they were born of caves, or that their race is that of the gods. . . ." Most accounts prefer the cave origin for the Chichimec peoples: "seven caves where their ancestors dwelt for so long and which they abandoned in order to seek this land, some coming first and others later. . . ."

The first six groups that left would play varying roles in the Aztecs' rise to power. Four—the Tepanecs and Chalcans, with the people of Texcoco and Xochimilco—settled around the lakes in the Valley of Mexico. They joined people like those of Culhuacan, already established, who had kept the Toltec heritage alive.

The Aztecs were the last to leave the caves, "due to a divine command." An old manuscript pictures them dressed in animal skins and armed with bows and arrows, setting out to follow the four priest-chiefs who bore the image of their god, Huitzilopochtli, on their backs. They roamed in dry country. One chronicle describes it as "a fearsome place" of thorny plants, of bears, jaguars, pumas, and serpents. At night when the wanderers rested, Huitzilopochtli spoke to the priests in dreams, cajoling, ordering, demanding what he would have. The priests related his wishes. The Aztecs obeyed.

From their tedious journey they remembered "great hardships," said Durán: "famines, plagues, thirst, tempests, wars, locusts, and hailstorms." Today the exact route remains unclear; places of battle are uncertain; dates are vague. The group seems to have been a fluid one, with some people breaking away to remain in a tempting place and some settled folk joining the migration.

If the Aztecs fought an enemy, their priests probably sacrificed prisoners; and if they remained in one place for a time they first built a temple. When this "was ready to receive the coffer in which their god was carried," wrote Durán, "they planted maize, chilli—which is like pepper—and other crops. If their god decreed a good harvest, then they reaped; if he determined otherwise, they abandoned the fields." Clearly the Aztecs had learned skills beyond those of hunting and gathering wild foods, but repeatedly at Huitzilopochtli's command they moved on.

Eventually they stopped near Tula, by now apparently in collapse. There by divine order they dammed a river to see what their destination held in store. The water formed a great lagoon, reported Durán: "The Aztecs planted willows, cypresses, and poplars. They filled the banks with rushes and reeds, the lake began to swell with all kinds of fish. Water fowl appeared. . . ." The people wanted to stay. A long prayer to their deity closed: "Let the pilgrimage end here so the Aztecs may now repose / And rest from their hardships!" But, said Durán, their wrathful god thundered, "Are they by chance mightier than I? Tell them I will take vengeance against them . . . so they will not dare to give opinions. . . . They must learn that they are to obey me alone!" He ordered

the dam destroyed, and the land turned "desert-like" once more.

It was here, near Tula, the god was born again. Some scholars believe Huitzilopochtli had been a hero-chief, deified after his death. Legend says that in his rebirth the god was born a warrior, fully armed, brandishing his terrible serpent-of-

DAVID HISER

Sun-filled gap in the rock of a mountain evokes a Chichimec origin myth. Most of the peoples of Mesoamerica believed that they entered the world from a cave—the womb of the earth. Symbolizing the primal birthplace, caves occur as a prevalent theme in Aztec art and religion.

Jesús Molinero Gonzáles plies the waters of Lake
Patzcuaro as dusk colors the day. Each evening he
takes his dugout canoe—a tree trunk hollowed with ax
and adze in age-old style—to fish in the lake.
For the Aztecs, who used nets, fishing provided
a significant source of protein at their island home.

fire weapon; he did battle with his sister Coyolxauhqui and a multitude of brothers after they plotted their mother's death. He defeated them all.

Evidently his mother symbolized the earth and he came to represent the sun; his sister, the moon; his brothers, the myriad twinkling stars. Every day afterward he rose at dawn to reenact his triumph, once again vanquishing his siblings and driving them out of the sky only to descend again into the underworld. The Aztecs were to witness this heavenly war each day and aid their god's triumph with blood sacrifice. Already they were his chosen people. Now they became his "Warriors of the Sun."

During these migrations Huitzil-opochtli gave his chosen ones a new identity: no longer Azteca, People of Aztlan, but Mexica. Experts do not agree on the derivation of this word or its implications, but it became associated with such greatness that it gave itself to the modern country, Mexico, and its citizens, Mexicans. (Not until the 19th century did the name Aztecs come into common use again.) In bestowing a new name the god promised glory, and from the ruins of Tula the poor Mexica could see what imposing splendor a past empire had enjoyed.

By tradition it was about A.D. 1195 when the wanderers entered the Valley of Mexico, to find a new empire beginning under Chichimec rule. These invaders had

Wielding a long-handled sickle, Jesús Molinero cuts chúspata *reeds from the shallows of the lake. After sun-drying the reeds for about a week, he will tie them into bundles for storage. For centuries Indians have used reeds to weave such items as baskets, hats, and fire fans. A mat "throne," the* icpalli, *served Aztec rulers. At left, a village woman makes a small* petate. *While weaving, she regularly pounds the reeds with a stone to keep them flattened and smooth.*

settled down, intermarried with survivors of Tula, conquered most of the valley, and established their capital at Tenayuca.

Recently a drive north from the center of Mexico City took my daughter, Ann, and me across what was once the northern part of Lake Texcoco to the ancient shoreline and into a quiet suburb. There the heart of Tenayuca, its great pyramid, still stands. We climbed the steep steps and stood where twin temples had graced its top. In Chichimec times this architectural concept was new to the valley. The Mexica adopted it, and the last three of the six or seven superimposed temple-pyramids of Tenayuca are Mexica construction, honoring Tlaloc and Huitzilopochtli.

Ann and I tried to imagine the extent of the old city, now hidden under small houses and neighborhood shops, but her eyes kept returning to the sight just below. "There're snakes *everywhere*," she said. A masonry wall of undulating serpents flanks the pyramid base on three sides. Nearby, other snakes arch their necks above spiral coils. Serpents carved in relief adorned walls at Tula; the early Chichimecs and the Mexica kept this motif. We know little of the Mexica's early experiences at Tenayuca, but they returned in the flower of their own empire to make the old city their own.

Before 1300 the ragged band reached a steep hill called Chapultepec near the western shore of the lake and settled there. As Mexico's archaeologist-and-diplomat Ignacio Bernal says, "Rapidly, they acquired a well-deserved reputation of being quarrelsome, cruel, unfaithful to their word, and women-stealers." People of the older city-states that ringed the lakes did not welcome them—understandably.

A Mexica chronicler recalled: "And their neighbours, when they saw the growth in their numbers, began to be troubled, and to make war upon them, with the intention of destroying them, that their name might be no longer known upon the face of the earth, and that their kind might not establish itself there." They were attacked and expelled from Chapultepec, but regained it because in their wanderings they had become as seasoned in warfare as they were tenacious and abrasive.

In the past, four chieftains called *teomama*—god-bearers—had served as leaders. Now, in the face of extreme danger, the Mexica elected one chief to lead the defense. He ordered the hill encircled with barricades, but these fell before a massive attack by the warriors of the Tepanecs and those of Culhuacan. "Although their leader was captured in the first skirmish," wrote Durán, "the Aztecs were not totally routed. Gathering the women, children, and old people in their midst and crying out to their god for help, they hacked their way through the enemy ranks. . . ." Although many escaped their chief was taken to Culhuacan and sacrificed.

A Mexica poet wrote of that day: "The margin of the earth was shattered / sorrowful omens hovered above us / the sky split open above us. . . . / But the Mexicans who escaped from enemy hands / the old ones waded to the center of the water / where the . . . reeds were whispering. . . ."

Few places in Mexico are as filled with heroism and tragedy as Chapultepec. Beginning with the Mexica's brave but futile stand, it has played a central role in the

---

Symbolic painting of Chicomoztoc—Seven Caves—records ancestral lore shared by the Aztecs and related peoples. Dressed in animal skins, the Chichimec tribes left the caves of origin on migration (indicated by footprints). Here Toltec lords in feathered regalia seek their help in war; "speech scrolls" signify dialogue. Last of the tribes to migrate, the Aztecs—or Mexica—set out to seek a promised land. Civilizing Toltec influence, and prowess in battle, shaped their fortunes.

Twin staircases—mark of large temples in Aztec style—
lead up the pyramid at Tenayuca. Wandering in search
of a new homeland as commanded by their god
Huitzilopochtli, the Mexica stopped briefly at Tenayuca,
where Chichimec settlers had built up a city-state. Later,
in A.D. 1428, the Mexica returned and took the city.

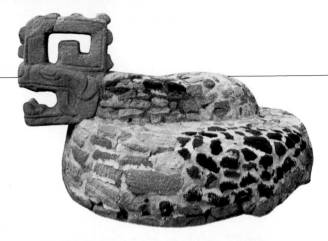

making of a nation. The great palace of Maximilian and Carlota, European rulers who failed to lead, crowns it and now serves as the National Museum of History. Here in 1847 the Boy Heroes, cadets of the military academy, fought to the death under the flag of Mexico—with its eagle-and-cactus emblem—rather than surrender to invading American troops. They live in memory as paragons of valor.

*T*oday Chapultepec is a place for a holiday afternoon. I've spent many Sundays climbing the hill for a panoramic view of Mexico City, or visiting the park below. There I've often strolled past families enjoying a picnic beneath trees already ancient when the Spaniards arrived, or watched lovers while away sunny hours with a boat ride on the peaceful lake. It is not easy to imagine that such a pleasant spot was the scene of so much misery in years past.

In losing the battle of Chapultepec the Mexica had lost their leader, their home, even their possessions. Friendless, in desperation they turned to their enemies. They approached the people of Culhuacan and begged for mercy. In their abjection they surrendered the banner and clothing of Huitzilopochtli to their new overlords—and this, says archaeologist Henry B. Nicholson, they would have done only in extremity. "It was as if they disowned their

Children play quietly beside a row of menacing snakes that guard the great pyramid at Tenayuca. A chain of these stone-and-mortar serpents flanks three sides of the pyramid. Two crested statues of Xiuhcoatl, the Fire Serpent (top right), sit coiled on each side of the pyramid, in alignment with the setting sun at summer and winter solstices. Below it, a carved stone skull, a reminder of the Aztec cult of human sacrifice, studs a pyramid side.

very identity as a people—as if they were losing their souls."

The Mexica asked for land that they might begin their lives again. A lord of Culhuacan granted them an area of volcanic rock occupied only by vipers, thinking the serpents would destroy them. In time, wrote Durán, he sent a delegation to see if the Mexica were finally dead. His envoys reported that their "fields were cultivated and in order, a temple had been built to their god, and the people were living in their houses. The spits and pots were replete with snakes, some roasted and others boiled." "See what rascals they are," the astonished ruler replied; "have no dealings and do not speak to them."

Perhaps these rascals were indeed protected by divine power. The Culhua lords hired the Mexica as mercenaries to

Food from the Waters

Wading in the shallows of Lake Texcoco, a fisherman surveys his catch—a net full of amarillos (left). For centuries, the lake has proven a valuable food source for peoples settled on its shores. Warriors carried the high-protein algae Spirulina (top right) as dried rations on campaign. Tiny water insects (center) lay their eggs on the stalks of reeds. Like the Aztecs, local Indians still collect the eggs (right) and cook them in patties.

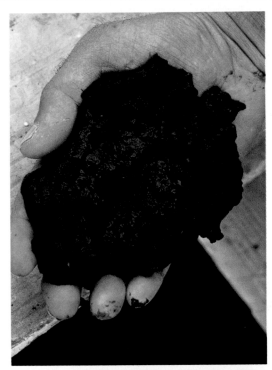

Paint and paper preserve scenes from the Aztec world. As recorded for the Spanish priest Bernardino de Sahagún, this drawing from a codex, or painted book, depicts a family crossing a desert. The man's bow identifies him as a Chichimec hunter. Where the wanderers stopped for a season or more, they planted crops.

help defeat Xochimilco. It was said: "The Mexicans supported themselves solely by means of war and they disdained death." In turn the Mexica bemoaned their reputation: "They seek us out because of their war, and the hardened shaft and the shield are our fate and our destiny." Destiny softened to let the Mexica trade in Culhuacan and marry among these people of noble Toltec descent. Mexica poverty had at least become genteel.

Huitzilopochtli, however, was never a deity to leave a situation pleasant. As Bernal says, he spoke "as the cruelest yet most agile politician. He never wearied, never halted; nothing satisfied him. For fifteen generations, his dreadful voice bore down on the people with tragic advice for violent action, without a minute of respite."

Now he told his priests to seek a "woman of discord," for the Mexica were not to remain here. Ever obedient, they asked a lord of Culhuacan for his daughter—to become a goddess and wife of their god. He sent the young woman, as beautiful as a "precious necklace." On her arrival she was killed and flayed and a priest put on her skin: an ancient rite of the mother goddess called Tlazolteotl.

When her father and other nobles arrived to honor the new goddess, the skin-clad priest was in the darkened sanctuary. A Mexica chronicle told how the father presented gifts "and after this, as he offered incense, he lit the censer and recognized the skin of his maiden daughter, and was struck with horror. He immediately cried out to his fellow princes and vassals, saying: 'Who are ye, O Culhua? Do you not see that they have flayed my daughter? . . . Let us kill and destroy them, and may they perish on the spot!' "

Fighting, the Mexica fled to the lagoon where they made rafts of their spears and shields to float the women and children to the other side. There they hid among the rushes. Durán says, "they passed the night in great anguish . . . with their women and children still crying and begging that they should be left to die there, as they could bear no more travails."

Even a god can go too far. Huitzilopochtli consoled his people. Next day they should seek the "place of the cactus and the eagle I now name Tenochtitlan," where their journey would end. So it came to pass, said Durán: on a prickly pear cactus they saw an eagle "with his wings stretched out toward the rays of the sun, basking in their warmth and the freshness of the morning." The Mexica "humbled themselves, making reverences. . . . The eagle, seeing them, bowed his head in their direction." The people "began to weep with contentment."

At once they set about making a platform of cut sod for their grass-roofed little sanctuary to their god, overjoyed that they had finally found favor with him. Their peregrinations had come to an end. The year, according to tradition, would be 1325.

The muddy islet of Tenochtitlan apparently offered little. It had lain unoccupied in a buffer zone by territory claimed by all three powers in the area, the city-states of Culhuacan, Texcoco, and the capital of the Tepanecs, Azcapotzalco. But it was easily defended, and the shallows could be exploited. A codex, or painted book, shows the Mexica of that period fishing from boats or with nets among waterfowl and clumps of reeds as they had done in Aztlan, their original home.

For a diet of survival they gleaned fish, frogs, birds, algae, and other foods from the lake. They traded these items to the people of the shore for firewood, timber, and building stone.

Four priest-rulers directed these first activities, for the Mexica had reverted to old forms of leadership after the massacre at Chapultepec. The dominant figure was called Tenoch, or Prickly Pear Cactus.

*I*n a literal sense the Mexica built themselves land. With pilings and reed mats they staked off plots in the shallows and filled them with fertile muck from the lake floor. These artificial gardens, now famous as *chinampas,* produced food crops in abundance. Perhaps it was not by coincidence that the god had selected his omen.

My friend Felipe Solís, Curator of the Mexica Collection at the National Museum of Anthropology in Mexico City, pointed this out to me one day as we looked at his treasures. He tilted a large organ cactus carved in stone so I could see the bottom. There a carved eagle stood on a cactus: the glyphic name. "It is saying, 'This is Tenoch's city,'" Felipe told me. "It also says, 'Tenochtitlan, Place of the Prickly Pear.' I believe this stone marked a boundary of the city. We have so many continuations here from ancient times. Farmers in the highlands still mark the corners of their fields by planting a cactus like this."

Following a pattern as old as Teotihuacan, the Mexica divided their city into four quadrants which symbolized the four sacred directions of the Mesoamerican cosmos. At the center stood the divine cactus and Huitzilopochtli's temple—at the center of the universe to the Mexica mind. This universe, however, did not run smoothly. Dissenters broke away and moved to a nearby island to develop a sister city, Tlatelolco. While the two continued to grow the balance of power in the valley changed, and with it their fate.

A tyrant named Tezozomoc had become lord of the Tepanecs and his capital, Azcapotzalco, rose to dominance. He terrorized his neighbors with force, and played one city against another with political acumen. The Mexica became his vassals, served him as mercenary soldiers, and paid him tribute in the old pattern.

But in time they chose a lord of their own, Acamapichtli, or Handful of Reeds. This youth was the son of a Mexica nobleman and a Culhua princess, grandson of the lord of Culhuacan. In Tenochtitlan an elder advised the new monarch: "You are now in command, / You have come to be the likeness of our god Huitzilopochtli! / . . . Behold that you have not come here to take pleasure / But to endure a new and heavy work. / You will labor, you will be a slave to all this multitude."

Alarmed at his vassals' presumption in choosing a sovereign for themselves, Tezozomoc demanded impossible tribute to humiliate them. He ordered a floating garden sown with corn, chili, beans, squash,

Overleaf: Landless refugees, the Mexica build chinampas—raised garden plots—in Lake Texcoco. One man pounds stakes into the lake bed as another lashes them together with vines. Others pour mud over layers of decaying reeds. Soon they will plant crops. Thus they enlarged and fed their island city, Mexico-Tenochtitlan.

Hill of the Grasshopper

On a sunny summer day, Mexicans gather at Chapultepec Park to relax and play. Above, a young couple sits by the weathered trunk of an ancient cypress, an ahuehuete. This was a park in Aztec times; portraits of emperors, carved in hillside rock, suffered defacement after the Spanish conquest. The present park covers about 1,000 acres in Mexico City, and the ahuehuetes (upper right) stand as living monuments to the Aztec civilization. At right, youngsters splash in a fountain fed by an underground spring. Springs like this once supplied the Mexica with desperately needed fresh water; they built a reservoir here. They may have

made this carved carnelian grasshopper an offering to their gods. Chapultepec means "Grasshopper Hill" in Nahuatl, language of the Aztecs. They first came upon Chapultepec before 1300 as poor and wretched migrants, they said. Settling here, they quickly earned a reputation as unwelcome barbarians. Their neighbors vowed to destroy them.

and amaranth. They delivered it overnight. A new order required a similar garden with a duck and a heron on their nests. "And at the moment that the raft with the tribute arrives . . . the chicks of the duck and the heron must come out of their eggs. If this is not done you will all perish." With the aid of their god the Mexica met the demand.

These fairy-tale miracles must have appealed to the small children who heard the saga, while boys dreaming of valor thrilled to the proclamation of Huitzil-opochtli: "Let my children suffer and weep now / But their time will come!"

Their time for revenge was long remembered: Mexica warriors had helped destroy Tenayuca and Culhuacan. As the Tepanec domain grew, the Mexica seem to have made independent conquests as well, such as Mixquic and Xochimilco. For them, one man as leader had been a good choice.

On his deathbed Acamapichtli asked that his successor be elected, a procedure that would continue until the end of the Mexica dynasty. A council chose one of his sons, Huitzilihuitl, or Hummingbird Feather, who married a princess from Tezozomoc's family. By this time the aging emperor was obviously well-disposed toward these useful subjects. "From this moment on," says historian Nigel Davies, "the Mexicans began to assume a special position among his many vassals." Pleased with the birth of a prince of his line, he reduced the Mexica tribute to a token payment of fish and frogs.

Life in Tenochtitlan was improving— people were building houses of stone instead of mud. Mexica warriors won victories in the warmer country near Cuernavaca, where cotton can be grown; and soft, luxurious new garments began to replace the scratchy fibers of the past. Tenochtitlan had become a significant military power in its own right and its sister city, Tlatelolco, was developing into a commercial center under the regal leadership of another grandson of Tezozomoc.

Chimalpopoca, or Smoking Shield, succeeded his father as lord of Tenochtitlan about 1417. He was still a youth in his teens. His grandfather helped him build an aqueduct to bring sorely needed fresh water from the springs of Chapultepec to the city in a lake of brackish—and polluted— water. Many of the old emperor's subjects were none too pleased. As Chimalpopoca continued a long war against Chalco, the Tepanecs came to Chalco's defense.

Yet while Mexica power increased, that of the Tepanecs waned. Tezozomoc's death after a reign of half a century doomed his empire. "It had been the creation of one man," writes Davies, "and could not easily survive his passing." Two Tepanec princes contended for the vacant throne; Chimalpopoca sided with the losing faction, and was killed. One tradition says the victor had him murdered, but another implies that he died a victim of his own kin, who thought him too weak and unwise for a Mexica ruler.

Nobles and priests would recall these stories, surely, debating policy and sharpening statecraft, to learn from their rivals and overlords. This was the schooling of princes.

Poor leadership now could not be tolerated. The Mexica had proved themselves as warriors. They had glimpsed what riches conquest and tribute could bring. Their little city was growing. The god had made promises he would surely keep. And the royal blood of Toltec empire-builders flowed in the veins of Mexica kings.

Chapultepec Castle, former residence of the Emperor Maximilian and now home of the National Museum of History, overlooks the modern city. The Mexica fortified this natural strongpoint in vain; about 1399 their foes overpowered them and the survivors fled. Nearby, in the lake, lay their promised land.

DAVID HISER

THE CITY

"With our darts, with our shields, the city lives....The flowers of the Giver of Life open their blossoms. Their perfume is sought by the lords: this is Tenochtitlan."

His was a name of strength, of biting force, of cunning and dread. He was Itzcoatl, Obsidian Serpent. In choosing the name, his forebears cast his destiny. The new king lived up to its implications and his reign swept the Mexica forward. He was a military genius and master politician who seized an opportunity and struck with deadly aim. Son of Acamapichtli but by a slave woman, he had debatable claims at most to Toltec blood. Chosen by the family, he became the first independent ruler of the Mexica, for his warrior predecessors were only vassal lords.

On his accession an orator declared that "Mexico-Tenochtitlan was like a widow, but the husband, the spouse, has been reborn. Let him come back and give it the sustenance it needs." Itzcoatl did not stop with sustenance. He gave the city freedom.

Preceding pages: Before their cathedral, holiday crowds mass at dusk in the Zócalo, Mexico City's main plaza. Still a great capital, the city rests on the ruins of Tenochtitlan, heart of the Aztec Empire.

EMBLEM, ABOVE: THE GOD TEZCATLIPOCA

Midway in his reign he styled himself Lord of the Culhua—in effect, Lord of the Toltecs, the title of highest prestige in his time. Relying on arms if not on birth, he claimed the role of heir to the dynasty of Culhuacan, and thus to the ancient empire of Tula; and he aspired to conquest and glory for his muddy little city. In later years its citizens would call themselves, proudly, Culhua Mexica.

Yet in truth the ennobled city was little more than a town of adobe with some buildings of stone or stone facings. In spite of its chinampas, steadily enlarged, it lacked adequate farmland and other natural resources that cities of the mainland enjoyed. The memory of hunger was still too recent to be dulled by time.

Self-consciously, Itzcoatl—man of clouded birth, ruler of an expanding state, eager for grandeur—decided to alter the record of memory. He had the books brought together, pictorial manuscripts painted on bark paper or deerskin. As Mexica elders told Fray Bernardino de Sahagún: "The story had been preserved, / but it was burned when Itzcoatl was king in Mexico. / The rulers of Mexico made a decision, they said: / 'It is not wise for people to know the books, the writings, / for . . . deceptions will be established in the land, / for they are filled with lies. . . .' "

My friend Thelma Sullivan is an authority on classical Nahuatl, the language of the Mexica. When I asked her about the burning of the codices, Thelma's blue eyes flashed a knowing look. "I believe that this was common practice on the part of conquering peoples who wished to glorify their own traditions. I'm sure the Mexica were substituting their own accounts for older, quite different stories."

By revising their past the Mexica showed the resentment they had felt as Tepanec vassals. The tyrant Tezozomoc had ruled the Valley of Mexico with a single purpose in mind—empire. He did not relinquish his power even after becoming so old, a chronicle says, that attendants "carried him about like a child swathed in feathers and soft skins; they always took him out into the sun to warm him up, and at night he slept between two great braziers, and he never withdrew from their glow because he lacked natural heat." He died about 1426, and within two years the Mexica scribes could record the defeat of his capital with the conquest glyph—one that shows a temple collapsing in flames.

Itzcoatl's warriors had joined those of Texcoco and other city-states in the decisive campaign. Thereafter Tenochtitlan— with its sister city, Tlatelolco—maintained an alliance with Texcoco and a sympathetic Tepanec city, Tlacopan. Combinations of this sort changed from year to year as minor states vied for power, but this alliance would endure.

Two of Itzcoatl's near kinsmen had played important roles in these events. Tla-caelel, a forceful man in his thirties, would become a powerful "mayor of the palace" and adviser to the king; he took the priestly title of Cihuacoatl, or Snake Woman, which came to denote the second position in the realm. The vigorous warrior known to us as Moctezuma I served as a military leader. This familial union of leadership, brains, and brawn had made Tenochtitlan a powerful partner in the alliance.

*I*n overthrowing the Tepanecs, the Mexica gained extensive land holdings. In the next 12 years Itzcoatl conquered all the rival powers of the valley except Chalco. His forces swept southward to subdue Coyoacan and link that city to their own with a great causeway. They took Xochimilco and its rich province of low-lying chinampas and fertile soil on the slopes of the mountains nearby. At last the Mexica had the adequate farmland they coveted.

The lush chinampas of Xochimilco still grow crops for the city, today mostly in the form of flowers. It is a popular spot filled with leisure boats poled through quiet, dark canals. There families escape the traffic noise and smog of downtown Mexico City to picnic, buy souvenirs, and listen to mariachi bands in a whirl of floating sound and color. They return home laden with bouquets and tin cans of plants for their

Wind and Smoke

Fluid lines of a dancing monkey portraying the Aztec wind god Ehecatl suggest the movement and lightness of air. Unearthed during subway construction in Mexico City, the stone-and-stucco figure, an aspect of Quetzalcoatl, wears that deity's beaklike mask. Functional beauty survives in a delicate and intricate clay vessel. It still holds copal, the sacred incense burned at Aztec altars.

own gardens—roses, hibiscus, gardenias.

Nearby and to the east lies a town that preserves the chinampa tradition. I spent an afternoon there in late November walking the narrow paths between garden plots, crossing canals on log footbridges, and watching people labor at chinampa horticulture in all its stages, from preparation of seed beds to harvest.

A teen-age boy dredged mud from a canal into a flat-bottomed boat. A young couple marked a muddy seedbed into squares as a radio blared rock music. Later, with a seedling growing in each square, the stock would be cut out intact and shipped to market. A man dipped water from the canal to sprinkle young blooming plants.

One farmer smoothed the floor and sides of a seedbed with a plank. Dried cornstalks stood in rows along one edge of his chinampa. He chuckled at my question about the harvest. "More than one crop each year? I would be a rich man. We plant corn in March when it is still cold. January and February are also cold. Sometimes, not every year, there is much frost in spring and winter. It can kill all the plants—corn, flowers, everything. Then we begin again. Life on the chinampas is sad at times, but the land is rich. It feeds us, and trucks carry our flowers to all parts of Mexico, wherever they are needed."

One crop a year from this rich province was enough to increase the wealth and power of Tenochtitlan. Itzcoatl added conquests beyond the valley: Cuernavaca and neighboring cities, northern Guerrero— lands of the so-called hot country, yielding valued products such as cotton.

At his death, in 1440, Tlacaelel addressed the mourners, saying: "Now the light that illuminated you is extinguished, the voice at whose sound all this kingdom moved is still, and the mirror in which all men saw themselves is darkened. Thus, illustrious warriors, it is not fitting that this

The Chinampas

Rich black ooze revives an old chinampa near Xochimilco. Claudio Galicia pours it in place while his helper watches from a boat loaded with more mud they scooped from the canal. Below, a farmer smooths his newly fertilized plot. Produce from thousands of chinampas fed Tenochtitlan; blooms from the few remaining now brighten Mexico City. At right, a boatman poles crates of living plants to market.

Açaith

yotomb

gectopa

aquexiatl

gezircuh

tenuch

xomimih

socoyul

xincpak

atotoh

tenochtitlan

colhuacan. pueblo.

tenayucan. pueblo/

kingdom be left in obscurity; may another sun rise to give it light. . . ."

That sun proved to be Moctezuma I, nephew of Itzcoatl, half brother of Tlacaelel, a member of the inner council of four. It became settled custom to choose a ruler from this council, and probably Tlacaelel's preference carried weight. The chroniclers often cite eloquent orations as his very words. Eloquence was greatly respected, and the word translated as king, *tlatoani*, literally means "he who speaks."

The new ruler's name did not belie his own force and skill. Moctezuma—Motecuhzoma, in the most correct version—means Angry Lord. His other name, Ilhuicamina, refers to one who shoots his arrow at the skies. He would lead his nation toward power that later stretched from the Gulf of Mexico to the Pacific.

Durán reports his coronation: "The neighboring kings came to acknowledge the preëminence of the new sovereign and to acknowledge their subjection to this supreme monarch. They brought him great and valuable gifts of rich cloth, weapons, insignia, shields, fine plumes, and jewels used on such occasions by the lords to show reverence to one another."

With his kingdom's wealth increasing, Moctezuma would be quick to show reverence to its gods. His building program for Tenochtitlan centered on its major temple. The first shrine here had been a simple one. "Meanly, wretchedly, they built the house of Uitzilopochtli," an old account confessed. Chimalpopoca had probably made improvements, but now Moctezuma was determined to raise "a sumptuous temple dedicated to his name and to our other gods." Durán records his orders to his allies and vassals: "You well know you are obliged to serve him and I command you that as soon as you return to your cities you order your vassals to come to this work bringing the necessary materials of stone, lime and wood."

For sculpture he requested from Chalco "a few stones from their hills, the largest that can be obtained." Chalco, an enemy of long standing, rudely refused and war broke out; the Mexica took 500 prisoners. "These were sent to Mexico and on the day after their arrival, by order of Tlacaelel and the king, they were immediately sacrificed to Huitzilopochtli."

We have no eyewitness descriptions of the city in this reign, but it must have acquired some of the splendor that dazzled the Spaniards eight decades later. Bernal Díaz spoke of "buildings rising from the water, all made of stone. . . . like gleaming white towers and castles: a marvellous sight. All the houses had flat roofs, and on the causeways were other small towers and shrines built like fortresses."

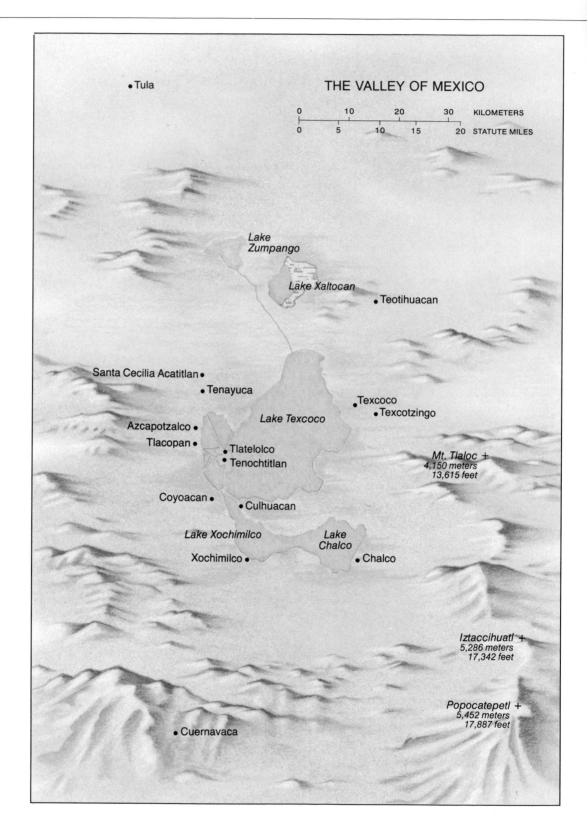

THE VALLEY OF MEXICO

0 10 20 30 KILOMETERS
0 5 10 15 20 STATUTE MILES

Tula

Lake Zumpango

Lake Xaltocan

Teotihuacan

Santa Cecilia Acatitlan

Tenayuca

Texcoco
Texcotzingo

Azcapotzalco

Lake Texcoco

Tlacopan

Tlatelolco
Tenochtitlan

Mt. Tlaloc +
4,150 meters
13,615 feet

Coyoacan

Culhuacan

Lake Xochimilco

Lake Chalco

Xochimilco

Chalco

Iztaccihuatl +
5,286 meters
17,342 feet

Popocatepetl +
5,452 meters
17,887 feet

Cuernavaca

Each quadrant of the city had an evocative name of its own. In the southwest lay Moyotlan, "the place of the mosquitoes"; in the southeast, Teopan, "the place of the gods"; in the northeast, Atzacualco, "the place where the water is stopped"; and in the northwest, Cuepopan, "the place of the road." Four avenues extending from the gates of the major temple precinct bounded the quarters, each of which had its own temple, administrative center, and principal plaza.

The quarters, in turn, divided into neighborhoods or "barrios." Each of these had a military school, an official to call out men in wartime, and a minor temple, a gathering place for the people.

In the residential areas, walls enclosing the houses of several related families opened onto canals or streets. "Some of these," wrote Cortés, "and all the smaller streets, are made as to the one half of earth, while the other is a canal by which the Indians travel in boats. And all these streets, from one end of the town to the other, are opened in such a way that the water can completely cross them. All these openings—and some are very wide—are spanned by bridges made of very solid and well-worked beams, so that across many of them ten horsemen can ride abreast."

Lacking horses or any other animals of transport, the people of Mesoamerica had to rely on two carriers: the human back and the dugout canoe. Anthropologist Ross Hassig has considered the constraints this created, using an estimate that canoes are 40 times more efficient than porters for moving bulk loads. Thus, he points out, the Mexica in their island city had a transportation system superior to that of any landlocked city—again they had turned adversity to their own advantage.

"We saw a multitude of boats upon the great lake, some coming with provisions, some going off loaded with merchandise," reported Bernal Díaz; in the great market of Tlatelolco, he saw a "host" of buyers and sellers whose "voices could have been heard for more than a league."

Apparently the Spaniards left the houses of the humble undescribed. The French scholar Jacques Soustelle writes: "In the suburbs there were probably still to be found the primitive huts of the early days, with their walls made of reeds and mud, and their roofs of grass or straw. . . ."

At the time of Moctezuma I the city was somewhat smaller in area and population than when the Spaniards first saw it. By 1519 some 150,000 to 200,000 people lived on something between 12 to 15 square kilometers, or 4.5 to 6.5 square miles. Its great causeways, canals, and avenues led to the center, heart of the empire.

There a high stone wall—some 440 meters to a side—enclosed the sanctuary of temples, a residence for priests, a ball court, and possibly arsenals. "State and religion combined their highest manifestations in this one place," says Soustelle, "and they gave a deep impression of their majesty: the white fronts of the palaces, their hanging gardens, the variegated crowds perpetually coming and going in the great gateways . . . and standing away one beyond another . . . the pyramids of the gods, crowned by their many-coloured sanctuaries, where the clouds of incense rose between banners of precious feathers."

Construction of the main temple went on, month after month, for subjects of Moctezuma I. Chroniclers mention two dates—equal to A.D. 1447 and 1467—for ceremonies that could have been dedications, but the building was never to be the

Mountains ring the high, shallow lakes of the Valley of Mexico, where the Mexica, like earlier nomads, found food and refuge. Alliance with Texcoco and Tlacopan increased their strength, and subjugation of Tlatelolco expanded Tenochtitlan.

Symmetry and order grace the hub of Aztec life, the ceremonial center of Tenochtitlan. Lesser temples flank the Great Temple with its shrines to Tlaloc and Huitzilopochtli. Near Quetzalcoatl's round temple, a dark *tzompantli* holds human skulls; a *calmecac,* or elite school, and a ball court complete the complex. Spaniards razed the city; consulting old documents, architect Ignacio Marquina created this model.

DAVID HISER

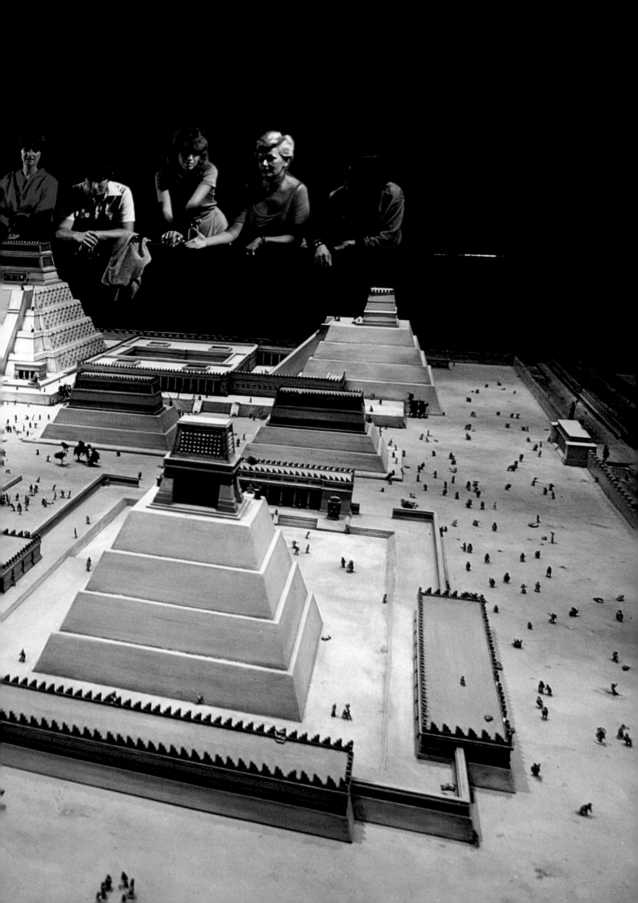

permanent triumph the ruler desired. Floods and the soft subsoil caused it to settle and tilt forward. Architects tried to correct this as they superimposed later structures on it, and the great temple the Spaniards saw had stood only 32 years—a codex gives it the date Eight Reed, or 1487.

Horrified by Aztec gods and human sacrifice, the Spaniards insisted that the images of Tlaloc and Huitzilopochtli be removed. The Indians eased them down the blood-smeared steps with a rig of strong ropes and took them away, probably for burial, to some spot unknown. Later the Spaniards destroyed the shrines, taking stone to build a cathedral. Time eroded local memory until tradition said the cathedral stood atop the ruins. Not until the early years of this century did archaeologists learn that the remains lay beside the great church, under various buildings. Since 1978 extensive excavation has revealed that the Spaniards did not destroy everything, and the center of Tenochtitlan is again a monument to Mexica splendor.

I stood near the excavations recently with archaeologist-and-architect Augusto Molina. "Look, do you see that this whole area is a slight rise?" he said. "All through the colonial period it was known as the Island of the Dogs. Mexico City had a long history of floods, and this was the highest point. Whenever the lake rose and flooded the city the dogs in town would come here and stay until the waters receded." Even after the Spaniards had taken the stones they wanted, there was enough rubble to cause a perceptible rise when they constructed streets through the vicinity.

Corrugated metal fences define the site today, and beyond those we entered a complex of partial walls and staircases from different building periods of the great temple, El Templo Mayor. "The city has always been sinking," said Augusto. "See, they used light volcanic stone called *tezontle* for the walls, but the stairs and balustrades are made of heavier stone—basalt." I noticed that the weight had pulled the staircases forward and down. As we walked further back in time and deeper below street level, the height of the walls increased above us.

Finally we climbed to the top of a complete staircase and gazed at the remains of two temples. A painted Chac Mool, possibly a messenger to Tlaloc, reclined in one; a narrow dark stone where priests had stretched victims for sacrifice to Huitzilopochtli rose from the other. The smooth plastered floors of both temples tilted sharply toward the steep flights of steps.

PRECAUCION
ZONA DE DEMOLICION
PEATONES CIRCULAR POR
LA ACERA DE ENFRENTE

Past is present in downtown Mexico City, where residents view their heritage in the excavation of the Great Temple, El Templo Mayor. Construction in Mexico has bared archaeological remains for two centuries.

Below, the greenish-black waters that underlie the city seeped upward over the flagstone courtyard.

Augusto pointed out three layers of mud in the stratigraphy—the deposit of three destructive floods. In another courtyard he showed me long wooden poles exposed below a stone altar. "They were ingenious," he explained, "sinking piles into the mud to stabilize the buildings. The Spaniards copied them when they built their city. The wooden piles of both look the same at first, but are really different. Aztec ones have the marks of stone tools and Spanish ones, of metal."

I was to visit the site many times in the next few months, and each time I shared the excitement of new discoveries with the specialists working there. Archaeologist Eduardo Matos Moctezuma heads the Templo Mayor project. One morning he jubilantly pointed to a new excavation at the foot of the staircase by the northwest corner of the temple of Tlaloc, from the last years of Aztec construction.

"We have a new offering," he told me. "This will be the 48th. It's a large pit lined with stone. Let's hope it will be filled with interesting things. You can follow the progress of the excavation."

From midsummer until late November, I went back often and sat beside Offering 48 as young archaeologist Francisco Hinojosa directed the delicate work. He and his assistants took samples of soil, measured, photographed and drew everything in the cache, and patiently excavated with dental picks and artist's brushes. As they moved meticulously down, level by level, I watched the contents come to light: 11 stone sculptures, each a painted effigy of Tlaloc, jade beads, copal incense, bones and the skulls of 34 children.

I recalled Durán's description of ceremonies performed each spring on Mount Tlaloc: "because on that whole sierra the clouds become cold, and storms of thunder, lightning, thunderbolts, and hail are formed. . . . the entire nobility of the land, princes and kings, and great lords. . . . took a child of six or seven years and placed him within an enclosed litter so that he would not be seen. He was slain by this god's own priests, to the sound of many trumpets, conch shells, and flutes."

The high priest collected the blood and "went to the idol Tlaloc and bathed its face and body with it. . . . if the blood of that child was not sufficient one or two other children were killed. . . ." In Tenochtitlan, meanwhile, a little girl "dressed in blue, representing the great lake and other springs and creeks," waited in an enclosed litter in the courtyard of Tlaloc's temple. When news of the completed mountain sacrifice reached the city, men raised the child in her litter to send her away. They took her by canoe into the lake to the spot of a fabled whirlpool where they slit her throat so blood flowed into the water. Then she was cast in; it was said that the whirlpool swallowed her body.

At the excavation I asked archaeologist Isabel Gutiérrez the ages of the children in Offering 48. "From three months to eight years," she replied. Surprisingly young herself and exceptionally pretty, Isabel told me about the fate of the victims.

"They were supposed to be killed for the god," she said; "at death they became his companions. Some here had a jade bead in their mouth to serve as their heart in the afterworld. It was good if the child cried very much at the sacrifice. Their tears represented rain. The children, the mothers and fathers—everyone must have cried. We found the skulls and only half of the ribs and an arm and a leg. The bodies were dismembered before they were placed in here."

Who were those parents, I wondered: commoners? Minor officials? And what became of those small remains? Were they scattered in the lake? Consumed in a ritual

Work in Progress

Urban change hems nested walls of successive shrines at the Templo Mayor. As the oldest temple sank in the boggy earth of Tenochtitlan, the Aztecs built another over it; they continued to stack later buildings. Colossal serpents—one shrouded now in a protective red tarp—adorned Tlaloc's pyramid. Conservator Ezequiel Pérez carefully brushes one of the basalt snakes with preservative (far right) and picks clean the sinuous curve of its jaws.

Mirror image of her model, archaeology student Mercedes Gómez sketches a Chac Mool found in the oldest of Tlaloc's shrines bared at the Great Temple dig. Color clings to the rough-hewn figure, the first and only one yet discovered with its vivid original paint. Aztec sculptors retained many Toltec forms.

DAVID HISER

Homage in Stone

Treasures from the Templo Mayor reflect the diversity of the Aztec Empire. Goggle eyes and drooping fangs identify a Tlaloc effigy executed in a style typical of northwestern Oaxaca. Idols, rare in earlier cultures, predominate among Aztec carved stone artifacts. Chiseled from an often-used stone called serpentine, a figurine in the abstract Mezcala style of southwestern Mexico probably came to Tenochtitlan as tribute—or as plunder offered to the gods.

feast? By sacred custom, it is clear, no one might taste the flesh of kindred . . .

In front of the temple to Huitzilopochtli we looked at another dismembered figure—this one sculpted. Coyolxauhqui, the slain sister of the god, is represented on a large circular stone. "She also had offerings buried in the four directions—one cache of female skulls was in the west. We have found another Coyolxauhqui stone beneath this one. It belongs to an earlier temple, and is smaller than this.

"And an offering found up in the temple confirms what we already knew—that we have the temple of Huitzilopochtli. It was an onyx bowl holding the tiny bones of a hummingbird. That is his name—*huitzilin* is 'hummingbird' and *opochtli* is 'left'—and hummingbirds were his *nagual,* his animal guise. As the sun he sat contented in his temple, facing west toward the sunset so he would go into the underworld satisfied and return next day."

I remembered that hummingbirds were the returned souls of fallen warriors.

"When we dug into the temple floor we discovered two more layers of temples underneath," said Isabel. "But to recover them we would have to destroy this."

Artifacts, bones—everything found at the Templo Mayor goes into the laboratory in a large house beside the site. By late November 1980, there were more than 4,000 items and new ones came in every day. Isabel and I walked between long tables crowded with Aztec discoveries. Many of the stone Tlalocs had been cleaned and the paint treated for preservation. Their large goggle eyes and fangs looked formidable. Beside them lay little human skulls from Offering 48. One was seven or eight. "He had already lost his front teeth, and see that one?" It was a female of five or so. She would have been crying. So small, so young. Neither of us spoke for a few moments; it was so easy to imagine the face.

I found other relics much easier to contemplate: faces carved from stone. "A partner of mine was digging an offering," said Isabel, delighted at the very memory. "She called, 'I found an Olmec mask.'" "I know," I interrupted; "you thought, 'she's got to be kidding!'" Isabel smiled. "When I came over and saw that it was true I still couldn't believe it. When she picked it up and brushed beneath it there lay a mask from Teotihuacan." "And then," I concluded happily, "neither one of you could believe it!"

People of such a short history in the long span of Mesoamerican civilization, the Mexica had offered their gods the ultimate gift—antique masterpieces from a past they held in mystical awe.

Some of the offerings can never be recovered. The chronicles speak of beautiful fabrics, tropical flowers, exotic feathers, and food of every kind. Temples and shrines were filled with gifts. Many came from far-flung margins of the empire, including sculpture from conquered peoples.

The toil of the Mexica and their vassals to produce such wonders and transport them must have been enormous. The Coyolxauhqui disk weighs some eight tons. The closest source for its andesite stone is a mountain 15 kilometers or 9 miles away. The monolith would have been dragged by ropes and rollers or floated on a raft to the great temple. The Spaniards never saw this great sculpture: It lay in front of the sixth temple, and the seventh was the one the conquerors knew.

"**W**e have recovered things the Spaniards never dreamed of," Eduardo Matos told me. "On the other hand, we are proving that what they wrote is often true. We have proved the location of the great temples, and in excavating them have brought to light the central story of the Aztecs.

"For us," he went on to explain, "the presence of these two gods, Tlaloc and Huitzilopochtli, reflects the basic economy of the Aztecs. It was not by chance that these two gods were present in the principal temple. Assured agricultural production, as well as tribute from warfare, was needed to preserve the Mexica state.

"Where we are standing was the physical and political center of the city of Tenochtitlan, the center of the Aztec Empire and the center of the colonial period. But it is still the center of modern Mexico City and the nation. Right here we have the continuum of the history of Mexico."

A short walk from that center lie the ruins of the sister city, Tlatelolco. Its great temple has also been excavated, showing the same sequence of sinking, tilting, and rebuilding through the years. Behind the series of temple stairs rises a colonial church built with tezontle from the ruins, and beside it stands a great stone structure. Its thick walls were cold on a rainy afternoon. Inside, a plaque is inscribed: "here Friar Bernardino de Sahagún wrote his History of the Things of New Spain 1564."

To anyone caught in the fascination of the Aztecs, this is a place to revere. It was here Sahagún taught Christian ways to the sons of noble Aztecs and the noble elders taught Sahagún, in turn, what they knew of their culture, history, and religion. That day's dismal silence was suddenly warmed by children's chattering and laughing through the halls—one room was serving as a classroom for workers' children.

If Tlatelolco and Tenochtitlan revolved around trade and warfare, the city of Texcoco became the seat of highland intellect. Its rise can be attributed to one man, probably the single most admired person in ancient Mexican history, Nezahualcoyotl.

His name means Fasting Coyote, implying self-control and religious humility. As a child he came to know the reality of physical privation. Under attack by Tepanec soldiers, he fled Texcoco with his father to make a final stand in a forest. When the king knew his situation was hopeless he said to the boy, "My dearly loved son, lion's arm, Netzahualcoyotl, where can I

Open lips of a stone mask, an offering found in a wall of the Great Temple, now speak of Aztec respect for the ancient civilization of Teotihuacan.

The Sculptor's Art

Again light meets the shell-and-obsidian gaze of a standard-bearer, blind witness to Aztec glory. Eight of these life-size statues line the steps to Huitzilopochtli's temple. Aztec masters of massive stone sculpture also fashioned smaller, finely tooled pieces. Red rings the grinning mouth of Xiuhtecutli, personification of fire. Special artistry distinguishes works of polished alabaster: a deer's head four inches high and an oversize dart point, both possibly baton ornaments, and a highly stylized ritual object in miniature.

take you to find some debtor or relative to take you in? . . . I am forced to depart from this life. I beg and charge you not to forsake your subjects and vassals, not to forget that you are a Chichimec, to recover your empire which Tezozomoc has so unjustly stolen, and to avenge the death of your afflicted father. You will make use of bow and arrow. Now you must simply hide in this grove, because your innocent death would bring to an end the very ancient empire of your ancestors." From the branches of a tree the prince watched helplessly as warriors murdered his father.

The Tepanecs and the Mexica divided his kingdom, and the boy began a series of wanderings, exploits, and hair-raising escapes that gave his contemporaries reason to think him a master of magic, aided by the gods. He learned to play each situation to his advantage, not an easy task in a time and place where alliances and enmity fractured and realigned cities like ripples in the lakes around them.

At times he found sanctuary with his kinsmen, the royal family in Tenochtitlan; and as a master diplomat he persuaded several city-states to join the Mexica in defeating the Tepanecs. In 1431 he was crowned, and two years afterward he regained his kingdom. To the Triple Alliance with the Mexica and Tlacopan he brought strength and statesmanship.

The Mexican scholar Miguel León-Portilla says: "In Nezahualcóyotl two distinct traditional currents converge, one from the old Chichimec invaders from the north and the other from the Toltecs with their teachings and doctrines attributed to Quetzalcóatl."

Nezahualcoyotl proved as brilliant as he was bold. A master engineer, he came to the aid of Moctezuma I after devastating floods inundated Tenochtitlan in 1449; to protect the city, he designed a dike or embankment of timber and rubble fill, nearly ten miles long. This also served to separate the saline waters of the eastern part of the lake from the purer water of the west. He planned an aqueduct with two channels so that one could be cleaned and repaired while the other supplied the people of Tenochtitlan with fresh water.

His architectural genius brought elegance to his own city. Nigel Davies says: "In its day, the palace was of almost Byzantine splendour; it had 300 rooms, and among its more notable features was the great council chamber, with its throne of gold, encrusted with turquoise." There were halls of judgment, quarters for the sovereign's guard, offices for dealing with tribute. Courtyards and gardens were interspersed among them. "A special patio was set aside as a kind of university, where poets, philosophers and historians taught, and close by were the royal archives." Here the sages of Texcoco fostered a cultural renaissance that glossed Toltec traditions.

*I*t is probably this aspect of Nezahualcoyotl that is remembered best, for he was a poet and philosopher in his own right. He did not approve, it seems, of the Mexica bent for mass sacrifice; he turned increasingly to an omnipotent spirit he called "The Lord of the Everywhere." In deference to his allies he built twin temples to Tlaloc and Huitzilopochtli, but he also constructed a temple honoring his own god. No images could represent this deity, whose home, he said, could not be fixed.

In praise he said: "God, our Lord, is invoked everywhere. / Everywhere is He venerated. / It is He who creates things, / He creates himself: God."

On the inevitability of death he wrote: "I, Nezahualcóyotl, ask myself / If perchance we take root in the earth: / We are not here for always, / But only tarry for a short while. / Though it be of jade it will be shattered, / Though it be of gold it will break, / Though it be of quetzal feathers it will come apart. / Nothing lasts for ever on this earth, / But is only here for a little."

Accepting life, he said: "Where can we go / Where death does not exist? / But for this shall I live weeping? / . . . Even princes are born to die. . . ."

As a lawmaker he was just, if stern, and his code became a model. He had his own son put to death for adultery. Once he fell into flagrant transgression—he sent the husband of a beautiful woman to certain death in battle, then took her as his own wife.

Yet to his subjects he was benevolent. A chronicle says: "He was a pious man with the poor, the sick, widows and the aged, and much of his rents he spent in feeding and clothing the needy, especially in years of famine . . . in such years he would never sit down to eat until all the poor had been fed. . . ." By customary law a man who took corn from another's field, even if only seven ears, incurred the penalty of death. As a desperate fugitive the young prince had run that risk; as a ruler, "to excuse the poor," he ordered corn and other seeds planted along roads and paths for anyone's taking.

In his province corn and other crops grew on the mainland, for the lake there was too salty to support chinampas, and terraces utilized steep terrain. Nothing remains of the old city, for the modern Texcoco covers the site, but something of the old works and terraces can be seen at one of Nezahualcoyotl's great projects, on the small mountain of Texcotzingo.

Early on a summer morning, art

With deliberate care, Guillermo Ahuja extracts a shell, part of a Tlaloc offering, from a vessel discovered at the Great Temple (top). Jade beads and shells filled the clay vase, which portrays Tlaloc's consort, the goddess Chalchiuhtlicue. Eduardo Matos Moctezuma, chief of the dig, watches María Luisa Franco paint preservative on a standard-bearer at Huitzilopochtli's pyramid.

BOTH BY DAVID HISER

83

Gifts for the Rain God

Leaning into his labor, Ezequiel Pérez scrapes grime from a wide-eyed Tlaloc effigy, one of eleven found buried with children's skulls and bones in Offering 48 at the Great Temple. The Aztecs thought young children suitable offerings at Tlaloc's great feast in the season of sprouting maize; their tears symbolized rain. At the northwest corner of the temple, a hard hat lowers mortar to another workman. Aztec masonry survives in floors and walls, but skillful patching repairs cracks and sets loose stones.

historian Richard Townsend and I climbed past prickly pear cactus, fig, and apple trees in fruit to the broad path that encircles the hill. "Nezahualcoyotl had another palace on the side of this mountain," Dick told me. "He kept an aviary of imported birds, as well as exotic flowers and tropical plants, and he had a royal hunting ground. The whole mountain was a garden of the empire's flora and fauna." The rainy season had brought its blessing. Lavender morning glories unfolded their blossoms; jade plants the size of small trees grew everywhere, their waxy green leaves edged in scarlet. And lilies bloomed the color of blood, the texture of velvet.

A masonry channel once ran beside the walkway, and spilled cool water into several pools for ritual bathing and purification. Shrines held sculptures in Nezahualcoyotl's time, and steps still lead visitors to the ruins of a building on the flattened mountaintop. "This hill was designed as a microcosm of the great rain-producing mountains of the highlands, and it was also a model of the empire," Dick explained. "The art and architecture served as religious symbols to show the relationship between the people and the lifegiving forces of the earth and sky. Texcotzingo was a small universe."

When we paused at one shrine carved from the living rock, Dick said, "Over there is an aqueduct Nezahualcoyotl built. The springs that feed the system are on Mount Tlaloc." That loomed as dark as a dreaded promise in the distance. Far below us farmers plowed the old terraces or worked in fields already sprouting a tender green. "Crops largely depended on seasonal rain," Dick went on. "Nezahualcoyotl's system irrigated his gardens and supplied drinking water for his palace, and took care of domestic use in the towns, including small household gardens. It couldn't provide for all the kingdom's farmland."

A small village lay at the foot of Texcotzingo; not far away, the modern city of Texcoco, and stretching in front of it miles of yellow-brown flats—the ancient lakebed. In the distance we could see the gleaming towers of Mexico City. We sat on the stone seat carved beside a ritual bath. It is where the ruler came to rest and contemplate, to walk the path of this small world on a mountain and ponder his life, his god, and perhaps his necessary alliance with the distant city of Tenochtitlan shimmering in the broad lake. Within the empire his devotion to art and intellect could not have differed more from the Mexica devotion to war, or his exalted god from the deities that controlled his allies.

"*T*he great twin temples of Tenochtitlan are really a Mexica metaphor," Felipe Solís explained to me once. "Tlaloc is the god of rain. Huitzilopochtli is the god of war but also the sun. Together they are water and fire, exact opposites. This duality of opposites said 'war.' That was the central idea of their religion.

"Tlaloc was an ancient god," Felipe continued. "He was the god of the peasants, the farmers. Remember, Huitzilopochtli never spoke to the people, only to the priests. He was the god of the elite."

In reality Huitzilopochtli was a tribal god with aspects of the supreme deity Tezcatlipoca, the eerie "Smoking Mirror." Durán says: "This [mirror] indicated that Tezcatlipoca could see all that took place in the world with that reflection." He was omnipotent, and forever young. He was the dreaded Lord of the Night. He was beyond all human alliances, The Enemy On Both Sides. He provoked wars; he brought

Santa Cecilia Acatitlan glows at dusk. Giant braziers frame the reconstructed sanctuary near Tenayuca, and a sacrificial stone at the entry recalls bloody Aztec rituals. Spanish invaders destroyed thousands of these small village temples.

DAVID HISER

87

Three Ages Today

Floodlit ruins of the pyramid of Tlatelolco, commercial center and marketplace of the empire, yield to a Spanish church and a housing complex at the Plaza of the Three Cultures in Mexico City. Here Aztec, colonial, and contemporary styles merge.

down mortal realms and rulers. An ancient text describes his arbitrary might: "Our lord . . . places us in the palm of his hand. / He rolls us about; / like pebbles we roll, we spin. / He tosses us about. / We make him laugh; he mocks us."

As the divine arch-sorcerer he haunted the night in phantom disguises. He was the giver of life who also took it away, sending down blight and plague, roaming the land causing strife and slaughter,

mocking his people with a laughing cry, bestowing riches or disaster on whim. Durán says the Mexica performed ceremonies to him: "Then all prostrated themselves, weeping, invoking the darkness of the night and the wind, begging not to be forsaken, forgotten, or killed, begging that the labors of this life be alleviated."

Did Nezahualcoyotl dream of ending the bloody cults of his time? If so, he could ponder the legend of Quetzalcoatl, the

priest-king and reformer who incurred the wrath of Tezcatlipoca—it was Tezcatlipoca who drove him and his followers from Tula, that earlier center of empire and intellect, and worked its downfall.

And now, just as the god had awarded the Mexica victories, empire, and riches and allowed them their great capital, he would nearly destroy all he had bestowed with a divine force "invisible as the Night, impalpable as the Wind."

The Poet King

Beckoning residents to cherish their Aztec heritage, a larger-than-life bronze statue of poet-king Nezahualcoyotl reigns over the entrance to Texcoco. Ruler of that city for forty years, Nezahualcoyotl contributed to the power of the Mexica by advising their monarchs and planning construction of Tenochtitlan's aqueduct and dike. At Texcoco he enjoyed a huge palace, a menagerie, and fantastic gardens famed in his time. Tourists can still view terraced fields from his ritual bath and seat at Texcotzingo (left), but little else remains of his center of learning and philosophy. His own words ring true for the empire he helped to build: "Nothing lasts for ever on this earth, / But is only here for a little."

91

THE EMPIRE

"That is why we were born!
That is why we go to battle!
That is the blessed death
which our ancestors extolled!"

The Mexica had found harmony with the gods. Early in the reign of Moctezuma I the movements of the cosmos, the Mesoamerican universe, and the bountiful cycles of the earth blessed the Mexica with power, riches, and elegance. Military might assured their dominant role in the highlands. Quite possibly the lord of Tenochtitlan sent his servants to the ruins of Tula to search its temples and altars for treasure: greenstone and turquoise jewels, buried in sacred places; carvings that might be stripped from sagging walls to adorn new ones. At the Aztec courts, literature, music and art soared to a new peak of creativity in praise of the people, nature, and the gods. It was then Tezcatlipoca struck.

His mocking vengeance was not swift and suddenly destructive. It spread slowly in unalterable stages until all its parts

Preceding pages: At an outpost of empire, Malinalco's rock-cut temple rises near a mountain crest. Perhaps rites of initiation for military governors took place in this shrine dedicated to the cult of the earth.

PRECEDING PAGES: DAVID HISER
EMBLEM, ABOVE: THE GOD XIPE TOTEC

totaled devastation. In the god's omnipotent hands nature went mad.

Locusts came like a dark, ravaging cloud in 1446, to eat the crops before they were harvested, but the Mexica survived on surplus grain from the storehouses. Then in 1449 Lake Texcoco rose, flooding the whole of Tenochtitlan. It was at this time that Nezahualcoyotl engineered the long dike just east of the city to protect it against future inundations. Autumn cold came early in 1450, bringing a heavy snowfall; many of the flat-roofed houses collapsed under the load. Frosts killed not only immature corn and other crops but trees as well. Again the Mexica turned to grain saved from previous years.

Unfortunately, the next autumn brought the same killing frosts before harvest, and hunger increased. Now supplies of corn became exhausted and many poor folk, especially the old, died of hunger. Then nature swung to another extreme.

Scorching droughts shriveled the crops of 1452 and 1453, and springs ceased to flow. A prayer went up to Tlaloc: "Oh, the fruits of the earth lie panting; / the sister of the gods, the sustenance of life, / feebly drags herself along, / she is covered with dust, she is covered with cobwebs, / she is utterly worn and weary.

"And behold, the people, the subjects, are perishing! / Their eyelids are puffy, their mouths dry as straw, / their bones are desiccated, and they are twisted and gaunt, / their lips are thin, their necks pale and scrawny. . . .

"May it be your will, / may you, at least, cast a sidelong glance at the people. . . ."

Moctezuma opened the royal granaries in the provinces and gave the poor a ration—one large tamale a day—but after a year even these supplies were exhausted. Starving Mexica scavenged the lakeshore for frogs and snakes, the countryside for wild plants. Proud Mexica sold themselves and their children as slaves to more fortunate people, especially the Totonacs, farmers of the fertile Gulf Coast that had been unaffected by famine. A girl brought 400 ears of corn; a boy, 500.

The young who stayed became so thin, dry, and wrinkled that they looked old. Most of the people who were old died. But death struck down those of any age. And vultures, rare in the highlands, rode the wind in search of corpses.

Symbol of imperial authority, this jaguar faces the entrance to the sacred chamber. Its pelt, carved in shallow relief, lies splayed on a bench of stone.

Helpless, Moctezuma summoned the people. He distributed new clothing and a last meal, and said tearfully: "Till now, my sons, you have seen that I have done everything that was possible to preserve you . . . each one of you should now seek his own remedy." As Durán reports: "Weeping bitterly, the people began to leave the city. . . ." Some "fell dead along the way, together with the loads that they carried. All of this was something never seen before in the land." It was 1454, the year One Rabbit, and it became a byword—the year when people died.

The strongest who stayed survived somehow, and 1455 brought abundant rain and a bountiful harvest. That year also began a new century or "bundle of years," a 52-year cycle the exhausted Mexica greeted from the Hill of the Star near Culhuacan. When the cycle had begun in 1403, the Mexica were serving others as vassals. At its close they and their allies dominated the Valley of Mexico and lands nearby—and at this point the ancient name Aztecs becomes useful to distinguish the empire and its allied rulers from the Mexica alone.

There are still stairs and the ruins of a low platform on the Hill of the Star. I climbed it to stand on that ceremonial structure for a sweeping view of the valley. Suburbs and fields stretched toward Mexico City and Texcoco, cities that had lain in darkness that night long ago, while their people waited, torn with the anxiety that permeated Mexica life. Nigel Davies says, "The New Fire was awaited with anguish and dread, for, if the fire was not drawn, the sun would cease to shine and the world would perish—this fifth world known as 'Movement', which, as all knew, would one day come to an end."

With the blaze of the New Fire came new determination. The Aztecs would not starve again. According to Ross Hassig, they intensified their irrigation systems, and added chinampas until these filled more than three-fourths of Lakes Xochimilco and Chalco. As he says, this increase in productive capacity "widened the margin between feast and famine."

Yet who but the gods could control

sun and rain and frost? And would the gods give men food if they were not fed?

To supply the hungry deities with the human hearts they craved, the rulers of the Triple Alliance negotiated a pact with the cities of the Valley of Puebla-Tlaxcala: an agreement for perpetual war. Soldiers in these "flowery wars" fought solely for prisoners to be offered in sacrifice. The offering of individuals was a custom so ancient as to seem eternal; now Moctezuma decreed mass sacrifices, and declared that war from that time forward would be the distinctive occupation of his people.

In 1458 the aging monarch sent his armies southward against cities in the Valley of Oaxaca for a great expansion of the empire. Ignacio Bernal sums up such campaigns: "Like a virtual avalanche the Mexican troops fell upon the peoples, broke down their disorganized resistance through surprise attacks, captured their chief if that were possible, mounted the temple and burned it. This was the signal of victory and there was left only the work of dividing the booty, women, and prisoners, establishing a government submissive to Tenochtitlán, fixing the tribute, and marching off to a new conquest."

The armies of the Triple Alliance swept past Tlaxcala to take the fertile coastal lands of the Totonacs. Perhaps these tropical farmlands would save the allies if famine should strike the homeland again. Moctezuma's troops fought victorious battles in other provinces, and finally won the long-drawn Chalco War near the end of the emperor's life.

The Mexica pressed Tlacaelel to succeed Moctezuma I in 1469. According to Durán, the eloquent adviser replied, "But how can I be honored more / than I have already been? / What further sovereignty could I acquire than that which I have now? / None of the past kings have acted / Without my opinion or counsel!" The honor fell to a very young prince, Axayacatl, or Water Face, grandson of Itzcoatl. As he had

Cult of Empire

In the cool hush of the sanctuary, the author contemplates the central sculpture: an eagle, the bird of the sun. "Here," she says, "you feel totally set apart from the world outside—and you sense the power of the state that commissioned this work." Drumbeats may have rung here once. This teponaztli, or horizontal hardwood drum, a Tlaxcalan piece, depicts a great warrior with his insignia of plumes and weapons that include a sawfish blade. For a pre-Hispanic scene in a film made at Malinalco, a student actor strikes a smaller drum also of Aztec style.

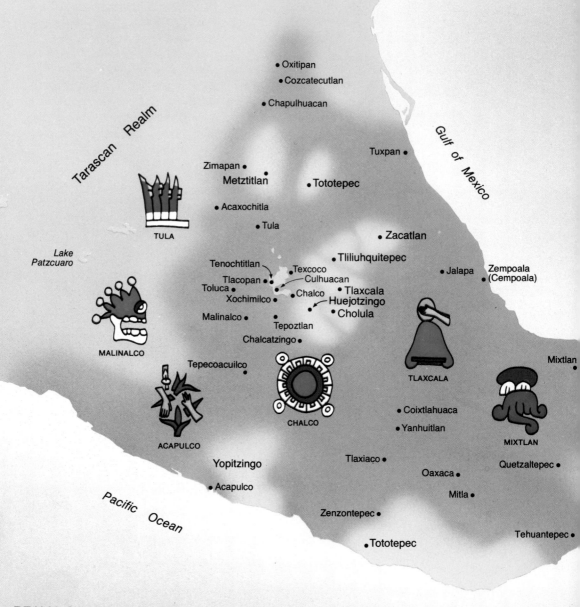

REALM OF THE AZTECS

| | Empire at its greatest extent, 1519 |
| | Independent Territories |

Map labels:
- Oxitipan
- Cozcatecutlan
- Chapulhuacan
- Tuxpan
- Zimapan
- Metztitlan
- Tototepec
- Acaxochitla
- Tula
- TULA
- Zacatlan
- Tliliuhquitepec
- Tenochtitlan
- Texcoco
- Culhuacan
- Tlacopan
- Toluca
- Xochimilco
- Chalco
- Tlaxcala
- Huejotzingo
- Cholula
- Malinalco
- Tepoztlan
- MALINALCO
- Chalcatzingo
- Tepecoacuilco
- CHALCO
- ACAPULCO
- Yopitzingo
- Acapulco
- Coixtlahuaca
- Yanhuitlan
- Mixtlan
- MIXTLAN
- Tlaxiaço
- Oaxaca
- Quetzaltepec
- Mitla
- Zenzontepec
- Tehuantepec
- Tototepec
- TLAXCALA
- Jalapa
- Zempoala (Cempoala)
- Tarascan Realm
- Lake Patzcuaro
- Gulf of Mexico
- Pacific Ocean

0 50 100 150 200 250 KILOMETERS
0 50 100 150 STATUTE MILES

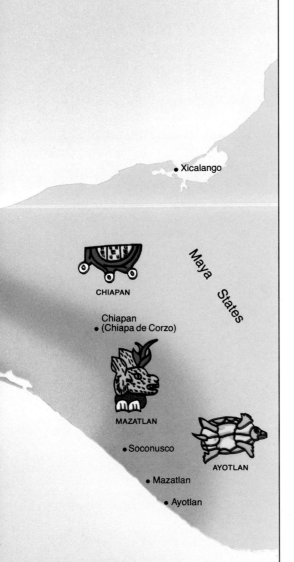

• Xicalango

Maya States

CHIAPAN

Chiapan
• (Chiapa de Corzo)

MAZATLAN

• Soconusco

AYOTLAN

• Mazatlan

• Ayotlan

advised previous rulers, now Tlacaelel guided the boy-king, but Axayacatl's most decisive conquest lay very close to home and it settled a long-standing rivalry.

Durán recounts that the king of Tlatelolco had married Axayacatl's sister, a poor skinny creature, raddled and feeble. He allowed her only a ragged mantle to wear and a mat in a kitchen corner to sleep on, preferring more beautiful wives—from less powerful families. To these favorites he gave the elegant clothing Axayacatl sent his sister. Discovery of her plight infuriated Axayacatl. Insults flew like obsidian-tipped darts between the two cities, and a lord of Tlatelolco vowed to "go kill those wildcats who are our neighbors." Tlatelolco staked everything on a surprise attack, and it failed. Tlacaelel shouted to his soldiers, "Our enemy lies right behind our houses. . . . Imagine that you are just brushing flies from your bodies." Axayacatl in person led the counterattack, slaughtering the men, capturing the women, and sacking Tlatelolco. Gradually, "their temple became filled with weeds and garbage, and . . . the walls and dwelling quarters fell into ruins."

The aggressive young lord proved his valor a bit farther from home by marching west and south to conquer Toluca, put down rebellions, and battle beside his troops for new territory. I visited one of his conquests, Malinalco, a town in a fertile highland valley subjugated in 1476. Axayacatl, however, did not live to see the great religious center built there. It fell to a brother who succeeded him, Ahuitzotl, to begin its construction in earnest in 1500.

The site sits near the top of a mountain on a man-made terrace with a commanding view. Artisans carved its main temple into the solid stone of the mountain by a kind of architecture in reverse, creating space instead of structure. A carved staircase flanked by jaguars leads to the entrance—a gaping serpent mouth. The threshold is the out-thrust forked tongue. One must walk the length of it to enter.

Inside, a bench cut from stone bears in relief the sculpted skins of a jaguar and two eagles, skins that curve up onto the wall. Another eagle skin spreads across the floor in front of a hole that leads into the mountain's depths. Why did Ahuitzotl order such an awesome shrine in a province already conquered?

"Malinalco was holy long before his time," Henry Nicholson points out. "It was famed for its sorcerers. It had been founded by Mexica who left the main group before Tenochtitlan was begun. I suspect that members of the imperial family governed Malinalco from 1476 to the end."

Those years had intervals of trouble, even of calamity. In 1478 Axayacatl had led 24,000 troops of the Triple Alliance westward to invade the Tarascan realm of Michoacan—a power much like the Aztecs in everything but language. A defiant army of 40,000 Tarascans met the allies in a two-day

war and almost annihilated them. On the first night Axayacatl could hardly recognize his great lords and captains in their new masks of sweat and dust. Durán gives the toll: "Those in the most unhappy state were the men who had sworn not to retreat; some of them were badly wounded, some by arrows, others by stones, others by sword thrusts, others pierced with spears. The king sorrowed greatly over them and felt great pity for the multitude,

Overleaf: Chalcatzingo, a highland settlement by 1600 B.C., flourished in Olmec times; it came under Aztec sway sometime in the reign of Itzcoatl. Corn and squash sustain it to this day. Successive cultures built dams that still check erosion, terraced the hillsides, and erected temples. Here the author examines a side of a pre-Aztec ball court, setting for a sacred game.

The Stone of Tizoc

Unearthed in 1791 by workers just off the Zócalo, this superb monument records the expansion of the empire under Tizoc, seventh ruler of Tenochtitlan. Mexica lords grip the hair of foreign deities, who bend forward submissively; 15 such scenes depict conquests by Tizoc, his generals, or his predecessors. Images framing them assert the cosmic nature of the Mexica realm: masks of the earth god in the band below their feet, eyes representing stars in a sky band above, and a stylized sun on the top. Ironically, Tizoc proved a poor general, a weak ruler. Consecrated in 1481, he died about 1486—and rumor said someone had poisoned him.

Waters of Life

Local boys sip water from a channel cut in the rock of Chalcatzingo in Olmec days. Nearby trails a vine, probably squash, as if growing from the runnel. Across the channel appears El Rey, *"the King," an Olmec lord enthroned in a stylized cave; raindrops adorn his headdress, and rain streams from clouds carved above him.*

from all the nations, that lay dead upon the field." When the allies retreated they had lost 20,000 men. Only 200 Mexica survived. Soon, after a reign of only 12 years, the rash young king died. Tlacaelel had probably died already. With their armies shamed and veteran leaders gone, the Mexica elected Axayacatl's brother Tizoc to the throne.

Durán mentions Tizoc with discretion: "his life was short and his deeds few." The new king marched northeast to prove himself in war and capture prisoners for sacrifice, the custom before each coronation. He captured 40 prisoners, lost 300 men, and, it seems, fled the field. Whatever he proved it was not leadership. To add to Mexica embarrassment, Texcoco was flourishing under the rule of Nezahualcoyotl's young heir, who had been crowned at age seven and was nearly as great as his father. Tizoc, Davies says, "preferred to seclude himself in his palace, showing little interest in public affairs and even less in wars. . . ." Such vacillating rule could not be tolerated. He died in the fifth or sixth year of his reign, probably from poisoned food.

Thus when Ahuitzotl, the third royal brother, put on the diadem in 1486 or 1487, he had every reason to reaffirm his nation's strength and destiny. By building the center at Malinalco he tied that land to Mexica royalty, militarism, and mysticism. The ceremonial center is a visual and spiritual statement of commitment to empire.

Richard Townsend has made a special study of Aztec public monuments. In the National Museum of Anthropology we walked around the so-called Stone of Tizoc and he explained the carving: 15 foreign gods bending submissively to Tizoc and his war captains, all with attributes of Huitzilopochtli. "It says Tizoc is the rightful emperor of the universe—everything on earth and under heaven." At another stone he said, "These two figures are Tizoc and

Ahuitzotl, slashing their earlobes and legs to let blood drip to the earth in sacrifice. This stone is Ahuitzotl's statement of legitimate inheritance of the throne."

If any Mexica ruler tried to conquer the world it was Ahuitzotl. Short-tempered even at his best, he flew into rages when things did not go his way. To avoid his ferocious cruelty both friends and enemies either catered to his wishes or politely declined his invitations. His ritual war costume was that of the ancient god Xipe Totec, "Our Lord the Flayed One," who wore the skin of a sacrificial victim.

To this day mothers threaten unruly children with his name, in Nahuatl or Spanish, and Dick Townsend told me, "When I was growing up in Mexico a favorite expression was '!Qué Auizote!—What a drag! What a disaster!' "

In his troops Ahuitzotl inspired fear and loyalty. He believed in forced marches, ambushes, and surprise attacks; and when conquest was accomplished he encamped with his men instead of living in his new subject's palace. Sensibly, he left the Tarascans alone; but his armies conquered coastal Guerrero and then the Isthmus of Tehuantepec, and reached the modern-day borders of Guatemala. I have visited many places conquered in these campaigns. One, in the Valley of Morelos, seems to have filled the Mexica with special respect and awe, for it held what they could never gain—a history both ancient and civilized.

*T*wo mountains, monoliths soaring up from the valley floor, mark a site and nearby village, both named Chalcatzingo. Just after a summer dawn photographer Mark Godfrey and I walked a narrow path that leads to ruins lying at the base and on the steep slope of one of the mountains. A burro's braying echoed time and time again from the craggy cliffs ahead. "Imagine the sound of a conch-shell trumpet here," said Mark. As we listened the song of a bird

At Tepoztlan

Hilltop temple honors a local god of drunkenness, "He of Tepoztlan"—and offers a view of fireworks on September 7. That night the villagers remember the god of pulque, one of a host known collectively to the Aztecs as the 400 Rabbits. Next day they celebrate the birth of the Virgin Mary; and in the evening they stage a pageant, re-enacting the conversion of their last pagan ruler to Christianity.

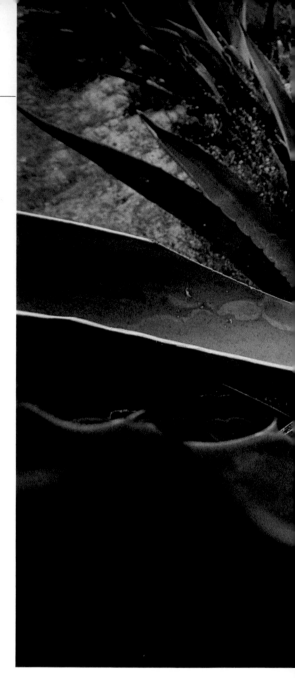

echoed in the same way, and when birds of its kind joined in, the air filled with different concentrations of the music. Yes. The mournful brays could have been the long, low notes played on conch shells; the birds' songs, shrilling flutes. Later the rolls of summer thunder evoked the deep rumble of Mexica drums, audible as far as six miles, at close range almost overpowering.

Surely such sacred music echoed here centuries ago. Archaeologist David C. Grove, who has studied the site since 1972, thinks it may hold the peak the Aztecs called Teocuicani, Divine Singer.

Chalcatzingo was already ancient when the Mexica brought it into their domain. Olmecs had adorned one sacred mountain's rocky face with carvings in low relief: plants, mythical creatures, jaguars, and men. A figure sits enthroned in a cave as raindrops fall from a scroll of cloud. Later peoples built temples, platforms, and a ball court, and painted murals in the lofty mountains' caves. They constructed steps and low platforms near these ancient Olmec figures.

I sat on the stone steps with custodian Salvador Velásquez as he told me about the carvings and their discovery: "There was a terrible storm in 1932 with as much rain and lightning as anyone in the village had ever seen. It was before my time, but I have heard the story all my life. Large rocks and trees came crashing down from the side of the mountain during the storm and left many places bare. After the storm had blown over, two men walked up here to see the damage. Don Sabino Yáñez was the first to arrive. He was the first to see the Olmec king and the other monuments—five in all. Who knows how many years they had been hidden by trees and fallen rocks—forgotten. Don Sabino and his friend notified the authorities, and an expert from Mexico City came. In 1972 archaeologists began working here."

Divine Plant and Divine Drink

Collecting juice from a maguey, Ascención Guernica Mejía sucks it from the center with a gourd; he carries it to open vats to ferment and become octli, or pulque, the only alcoholic drink of the Aztecs. They considered it divine. Ritual use excepted, rulers ordered death for gross abuse of it. A good vendor of maguey syrup boiled it to the consistency of fine honey; a bad vendor cheated and watered it down.

A smile spread across his face. "I was part of the crew and helped excavate. There were many burials with beautiful pots as offerings. And a curious thing. A small model of the mountain with stairs and everything, all carved on one large stone. Don Sabino is old now, but he still comes out to see the carvings he discovered. When there are no visitors here and I feel lonely, I go visit the king."

Mark and I also climbed up to visit the ruler and share the panorama his sculptor chose for him 2,700 years ago. I laid my face against the cold stone to duplicate the view of his domain. Far below, between us and the village, stretched fields of corn, beans, and squash. We gazed across the valley at the distant escarpment that defines the northeastern border of the Valley of Morelos. Beyond rose the great summit of Popocatepetl, jeweled in ice.

*T*o the Olmec, Chalcatzingo was a center for ceremony at least partially oriented to water and fertility. Rainwater flows into a stone channel, past the feet of the "Olmec king," and a carved squash vine seems to grow upward from the stream. Down the slope, two earth-and-rubble check dams from about 1000 B.C. divert the rushing waters to prevent erosion—the oldest manmade water system in the highlands.

Chalcatzingo also served the Olmec as a commercial and trade center. From that time on, whoever held the area controlled the crossroads of rich trade between the highlands and the coast. The name Chalcatzingo means "Little Place of the Chalca." By defeating that strategic region the Mexica had gained more than ancient gods for their growing empire.

It is difficult to imagine the details of Mexica ceremonies that took place at sites like these. Dick Townsend thinks that the cave-like shrine at Malinalco served for the ritual installation of military governors. Durán says pilgrims went to Teocuicani to

make varied offerings "—and to slay men." And eyewitness accounts of Ahuitzotl's spectacular dedication of the great temple in Tenochtitlan in 1487 describe the greatest orgy of human sacrifice in the history of the Aztec Empire. Ahuitzotl invited kings and noblemen from other cities, enemies and allies alike, to attend. Not daring to refuse, they duly assembled. Some authorities doubt this figure, but Durán says 80,400 victims formed four lines stretching far along the causeways into the city. "All the lords of the provinces, all the enemies, were watching from within the bowers which had been built for this occasion. The files of prisoners began to mount the steps. . . ."

The kings of the Triple Alliance, in full regalia, "assisted by the priests, who held the wretches by the feet and hands, began to kill.

"They opened the chests of their victims, pulled out the hearts and offered them to the idols and to the sun. . . . this sacrifice lasted four days from dawn to dusk. . . . Many priests went about gathering this blood in large gourds, taking it to the different temples of the wards and smearing the walls, lintels and thresholds with it. . . . and the stench of the blood was so strong that it was unbearable.

"The guests thanked the Aztecs for the favor and good treatment that had been given them, and they departed from Mexico bewildered by the majesty of the city and the amazing number of victims who had died."

Bewilderment soon changed to terror as Ahuitzotl's cruel armies swept more provinces into the empire. Attacks were deadly and swift, for he knew the strengths and weaknesses of each province. Gradually the Triple Alliance had become more a tradition than a necessity for empire, for Mexica strength eclipsed that of Tlacopan and Texcoco. Even Texcoco now made a significant concession to Tenochtitlan, yielding part of her time-honored share of tribute. And one subject town, Tepoztlan, spreads beneath a temple that still bears the glyph of the dreaded king's name.

The town lies deep within a horseshoe-shaped valley in the Sierra del Ajusco, mountains that border the Valleys of Mexico and Morelos. The volcanic sierra stretches roughly from Tepoztlan to Malinalco, and time has weathered it into a land of fantasy. Locals give surrounding peaks such names as Mountain of Light, The Three Marys, and Corridors of the Air. The eye sees what the mind chooses in these rocky precipices. Castles, demonic faces, crouching jaguars appear and magically change to other images with the shifting light. Fogs or long, slow-moving clouds stretch misty fingers to search mysterious crevices in undulating cliffs, then soften the soaring peaks to a delicate oriental landscape.

*T*radition and mysticism permeate Tepoztlan. One scholar thinks it was the birthplace of Quetzalcoatl, the deified lord of Tula. It probably came into the Aztec Empire during the reign of Itzcoatl, but glyphs in the mountaintop temple above the town refer to Ahuitzotl in the last year of his reign, 1502. A statue of the god Tepoztecatl, also known by the calendric name Two Rabbit, once sat in the sacred chamber. He was a local god of harvest and of pulque, an alcoholic drink made from the juice of the maguey.

The people of Tepoztlan once honored him and celebrated the harvest by consuming large quantities of pulque. As a supernatural hero-lord, Tepoztecatl supposedly freed the town of obligation to pay tribute to a nearby power long before they incurred a similar obligation to the Mexica. There is still an autumn festival, but it has changed through time.

At dusk on September 7, I watched from the terraced garden of an inn on a slope above the village. Townspeople and

Toluca, once a rebellious Aztec province, now sells its colorful produce at a weekly market as large as any in Mexico. Below, tomatoes and assorted chilis. The Aztecs happily distinguished different kinds of chilis by size, color, and heat.

A vendor displays green squashes and the yellow blossoms, to be fried or simmered in a famous soup. The toasted seeds also ranked as a delicacy among the Aztecs.

Corn: "Our Sustenance"

Guardian of the most cherished crop, the maize goddess Chicomecoatl—Seven Serpent—holds a staff symbolizing fertility. During Aztec times, various rituals surrounded corn's growth. The "great vigil" began with a four-day fast; then villagers cut fine young stalks and decked them with flowers. From the first, good cornland attracted Aztec armies beyond the Valley of Mexico with its marginal climate. Below, tassels crown the

stalks in August in the fertile Valley of Morelos, near the cone of Popocatepetl. Little changed since Aztec times, the corn crib called cuezcomate *stands about two stories high. Usually farmers let ears dry on the stalk before piling them into granaries. Since dried corn keeps as long as a year, it provides a reserve till the next harvest—or famine.*

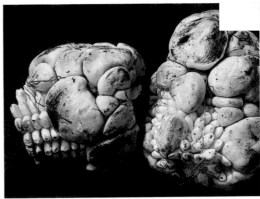

Fungus called huitlacoche, *or corn smut, spreads over diseased kernels in the rainy season. The Aztecs relished it; in the Valley of Mexico today it figures in soups, stews, steak sauce, or crêpes.*

visitors made the traditional 2,000-foot climb up a steep path to the temple to pay homage to Tepoztecatl. As night came in a pouring rain the mountains and sky changed to one plane of blackness. Then a waving line of flaming torches and lanterns suddenly appeared on the mountaintop, giving those of us below the vision of a fiery serpent suspended in the heavens.

For hours rockets arched and exploded above the ruin, answered by firecrackers and rockets from churchyards below. The storm joined the celebration with long shafts of lightning and loud thunder. Dogs, hogs, roosters, church bells, car horns, battling brass bands in the town square, and radios blaring loud music continued late into the night: bark, bang, bong, honk, oink. Cha cha cha.

It all began again before dawn, for mornings in Mexican villages never begin, they evolve. At first light one of the brass bands stood in the doorway of the large 16th-century church sweetly playing *"Las Mañanitas,"* the Mexican birthday song, for September 8 is the traditional birth date of the Virgin. It is also the traditional date of the baptism of the last king, also called Tepoztecatl, or El Tepozteco. That night saw a celebration in the town square.

"It is always staged by a few local families with a long proud history," a man told me. "They change it a little every year but the theme is always the same."

That night a group entered the town square dressed in fringe, feathers, and glitter. To the sound of bugles and drums El Tepozteco and his nobles mounted a plank-and-fabric pyramid. Below, men costumed as kings from Cuernavaca and other valley cities berated the ruler in Spanish for becoming Christian. Suddenly little-boy soldiers in bedsheet mantles and cardboard diadems fired volleys of arrows up at the defiant ruler. The missiles soared high into the air, paused; came hurtling down into the fascinated and suddenly scattering mob. In a moving speech in Nahuatl the king defended his decision, and through his eloquence converted the hostile leaders who confronted him. With history and religion dispatched, the people of Tepoztlan danced the night away to the music of a rock band in the square.

Such mixtures of myth and fact, ancient and modern, can be found in many parts of Mexico. Spaniards conquered the town in 1521 and added their gloss to its traditions while sweeping it into still another empire. The soldier Bernal Díaz remembered it as a place of "very good-looking Indian women and much spoil"— certainly valid reasons, along with copper mines, for Mexica conquest long before.

Usually the first Mexica visitors to an independent city or province came as traders, or *pochteca*. By the time of Ahuitzotl these entrepreneurs had made themselves vital figures in the expansion of empire. This king was quick to grant power and influence to whoever proved himself brave and self-sacrificing for the glory of Tenochtitlan. As spies these traders reported foreign wealth, terrain, defenses and military strength— many were fluent in foreign tongues, and Nahuatl was becoming widely known.

Devious, scheming, and secretive, they vowed to leave their hair uncut while on their mission; they slipped out of the city at night to travel armed, sometimes for hundreds of miles, gathering goods and information. They returned like stealthy shadows in darkness, laden with riches. In

Pochteca—*far-ranging Aztec merchants—proffer a finely embroidered cotton mantle of "eagle face" design to a lowland ruler in Xicalango, a port of trade on the Gulf Coast. They act for the emperor, to whom they will take quetzal plumes from the Maya area; they trade ordinary wares for themselves. Aztec merchants often served the state as spies.*

Cacao, source of the Aztecs' luxury drink cacahuhel, *grows on this small plantation in lowland Chiapas; workers scoop the seeds or "beans" from the pods to dry in the sun. Servants prepared the ancient potions with honey, spices, or chili. Sahagún's high-born informants said that too much "makes one dizzy, confuses one, makes one sick, deranges one." In moderation, "it gladdens one, refreshes one, consoles one, invigorates one." The drinker would say, over a frothy cup, "I take cacao. I wet my lips. I refresh myself."*

public the pochteca dressed simply, storing their enormous wealth secretly with relatives and bemoaning their great poverty. But while the city slept they dressed like monarchs to entertain one another in lavish night-long banquets. Pochteca were people even Tezcatlipoca could love.

During one long-term trading mission to Chiapas, a group of pochteca was attacked and besieged by enemy forces. When word reached Tenochtitlan, the king sent a rescue force southward with all speed. But on the march the soldiers met the elated pochteca returning, burdened with loot. They had taken their enemies' weapons, killed them, and added their valuables to their own bundles of riches.

One of the brave young warriors who had rushed to their aid was Axayacatl's son and Ahuitzotl's nephew, later known as Moctezuma II. He escorted the traders back to the capital; and at the palace his uncle heaped extraordinary honors on those triumphant commoners—the rights to wear gold jewels and fine mantles of specified design on certain holidays.

The usual rule of Mexica empire was that conquest followed commerce. Wealth once gained through trade then came as tribute. Illustrated lists detailed items and amounts demanded of each province. Traveling Mexica officials saw that tribute was sent; others in the city made certain it arrived. Durán writes of the goods that poured into Tenochtitlan: "Great quantities of gold, in dust and worked as jewels. Large amounts of green stones, of crystal, of carnelian, bloodstones, amber. . . . Vast amounts of cacao. Cotton in large bundles, both white and yellow. A bewildering amount of cloth. . . . Exceedingly rich mantles for the lords . . . all of them embroidered in many colored threads and enriched with the down of ducks. . . . handsomely colored birds. . . . Wild animals such as ocelots, jaguars, wildcats. . . . Great and small snakes. . . ."

His list continues with variations such as seashells and live turtles and pearls, amber, honey, fruits, vegetables, game such as deer and rabbits and quail, stone, wood, and "flowers of a thousand varieties," cotton armor, weapons, featherwork, and even centipedes and spiders. "Let one try to imagine all the products of this land and he will know what was sent as tribute to Mexico!" He adds, "Provinces that lacked foodstuffs and clothes paid in maidens, girls and boys, who were divided among the lords—all slaves."

At best such tribute in such quantities was difficult for conquered people to amass. For some it proved an extreme hardship. All shared bitter hatred of the Mexica and the burdens they imposed. According to Bernal Díaz, one ruler on the Veracruz coast, known only as the Fat King or Fat Chief, "broke into bitter complaints" saying the Mexica ruler "had taken away all his golden jewellery, and so grievously oppressed him and his people that they could do nothing except obey him, since he was lord over many cities and countries, and ruler over countless vassals and armies of warriors."

*O*ne of the most valuable items of tribute was cacao from tropical areas such as the Gulf Coast. The Aztecs used the beans as a kind of legal tender, and made a variety of chocolate drinks allowed only to the elite. It is still a valued crop, and in June farmers are busy at harvest at the town of Comalcalco, Tabasco. They spread cacao beans on large concrete pads in the hot tropic sun. Anthropologist Jeffrey Wilkerson and I visited a cacao farm where an attractive young woman welcomed us with a beaming smile. We walked into a dark grove of low trees laden with large pods. Taller trees shaded them. "We call those the mothers," the woman explained. "They care for the little trees and give them shade. Then the little trees give us cacao."

A teen-age boy hacked a pod open and

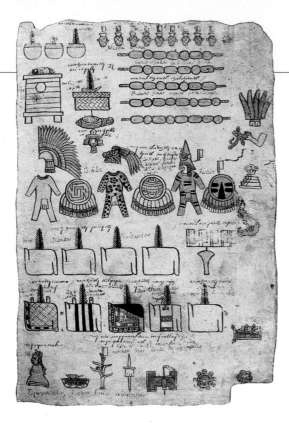

Tribute exacted by war or the threat of war offset any risks of trade in the Aztec Empire. Three official ledgers survived. In the margins of each bark-paper page of the Matrícula de tributos, glyphs record the principal and lesser towns of a province. The example above concerns Tepecoacuilco and 11 other places in the modern state of Guerrero. Tribute items, due at regular intervals, include (from top) bowls, jars of honey; a granary; copal; five strings of semiprecious beads; warriors' suits; plain or elaborate mantles. Numerical symbols listed units of one by a dot, or a finger; a flag means 20; a feather, 400; a bag with tassels, 8,000. The yearly totals elude all reckoning now; but if provinces failed to meet their obligations—a risky business, seldom ventured—their children as living tribute might spend their lives as slaves.

offered it to us. Each morsel inside was fuzzy, slippery, and deliciously sweet—nature's way of nurturing and protecting each bean. The woman laid a pod in her open palm and split it with one blow of a sharp machete. "To enjoy on your journey," she said. Astonished at her skill and delighted with our gift, we accepted.

Ahuitzotl's warehouses filled with such valued tribute as cacao and his treasury with gold, silver, and precious stones. The empire commanded more territory than ever before. He felt that he and his armies needed respite from long marches and hard-fought campaigns, so he busied himself with the growing capital.

*F*resh water had often been scarce in Tenochtitlan. At times during the dry season there was not enough to water the crops, and even small boats scraped bottom in drying canals. To assure an abundant supply in all seasons Ahuitzotl devised a plan to dam a great spring in Coyoacan and bring water to the city by a new aqueduct. The lord of Coyoacan had little choice but to agree. However, as Durán reports, he gave public warning: "The water of that spring was plentiful and when it filled the lake it had no outlet for its overflow and could inundate Mexico." In a rage at such impertinence, Ahuitzotl ordered the ruler strangled: "This can be an example for others who might give advice when they had not been asked."

A huge labor force like "ants on an ant heap" dammed the spring and built a conduit two leagues long. Sovereigns and nobles welcomed the first flow of water with orations and child sacrifice, greeting Tlaloc and his consort, goddess of springs, lakes and rivers, metaphorically called "She of the Jade Skirt." "Precious lady," said the chief priest, "you come your way in most welcome fashion."

All too soon houses were submerged in a flood, crops were ruined, and people fled their homes. Just as Moctezuma I had called Nezahualcoyotl to dam the lake, now the distraught Ahuitzotl sought advice from wise Nezahualpilli, his son, on how to dam the flow. The Texcocan denounced his fellow monarch for killing the lord of Coyoacan: "you have offended and sinned against the gods . . . the dams should be demolished . . . the water should follow its previous course. . . ." Nezahualpilli also ordered divers to block the spring with stones. Tenochtitlan began rebuilding "with better constructions, more original and elegant in style." Ahuitzotl died in 1502, and a chronicle says he never fully recovered after striking his head on a lintel while trying to escape the flood.

The Mexica buried him with more pomp and splendor than they had shown any previous ruler. From the array of royal princes, sons of the three brothers who had ruled, the electors agreed to choose a mature leader—not a "raw youth or a dotard," said the lord of Tlacopan. Although the empire now stretched from the Pacific to the Gulf and southeastward to Guatemala, it was a vulnerable domain. Within its widespread borders lay territories of unconquered people. The sovereigns of the Triple Alliance and their nobles knew the dangers of rebellion, or the possibility of attack from enemy alliances. They chose the 34-year-old royal commander of one of the armies, Moctezuma Xocoyotzin, or the Younger, because "as well as being most valiant, he was grave and temperate, so that people marvelled when they heard him speak . . . with such wisdom and aptitude that all wondered; and thus before becoming king, he was feared and revered."

Bernal Díaz describes Moctezuma II as "of good height and well proportioned, slender, and spare of flesh, not very swarthy. . . ." With the self-command of a prince, he could seem "cheerful" as well as grave and severe "when necessary."

Son, great-grandson, and nephew of kings, Moctezuma took his royal status with extreme seriousness. He reversed his predecessor's policy of promotion for merit, and dismissed all his appointees. He banned all commoners from the court, and decreed that nobles alone could serve in high positions. He led his troops in the field—in one battle he wore such splendid feathers and rich trappings he appeared to be a soaring bird in flight. Still, although his armies conquered new territory, his policy for the empire was one of consolidation. No doubt he thought he was lessening the possibility of rebellion.

But, as an 18th-century historian saw, the "oppression which he made his vassals feel, the heavy burdens he imposed on them, his own arrogance and pride, and excessive severity in punishments, disgusted his people. . . ." Nigel Davies notes that Ahuitzotl, for all his violent temper, had been warmhearted and affectionate with his subjects. "Moctezuma by contrast was colder and more calculating; in his treatment of inferiors almost a martinet, and in his religious zeal nearly a bigot."

*I*mmediately after his election the council had found him sweeping a temple. He spent long hours in his palace meditating or in the temples praying and performing sacrifices. He now had millions of subjects to control, and hundreds of gods to appease. At the coronation Nezahualpilli had reminded his new peer of his obligation to the sacred powers of the earth: "You must care for the mountains and deserts where the sons of god go to do penance and to live in the solitude of caves. You must care for the divine springs and fountains." By implication this shrewd adviser had spoken of the Toltec priest-god, Quetzalcoatl, who, as a heavenly body, overlooked the Aztec empire and promised to return. "You must go out and watch the stars, to know their course and their signs, influences and portents. Above all, you must take note of the morning star. . . ."

One Provincial Town: A Sample of Aztec Tribute

Market day in Xochitlan, a highland Totonac town without an access road, reveals aspects of life in the Aztec Empire. Farmers trudge a dozen miles or more on slippery trails, their tumplines securing bundles of goods; textile traders may walk three or four days to get here. At left, a thoughtful townswoman inspects crockery from higher country with good clay; at right, people gossip or haggle over foodstuffs and bundles of cotton garments. A tile roof shelters the "covered market" (background, right) for meat and fabrics. Under the empire, this town paid tribute in cotton cloth and in tiny, fiery "bird-beak" chilis (below).

THE SOCIETY

"We go, we walk, along a very narrow road on earth. On this side is an abyss, on that side is an abyss....One goes, one walks, only in the middle."

"They had such a different happiness," Felipe Solís said once when we were discussing Mexica life. "A different concept. Not the way we know happiness. Their lives were so filled with apprehension. I believe that only within the walls of their homes could they relax a little, enjoy family life, find a little pleasure."

The rigid structure and ultimate purpose of each Mexica life were proclaimed at birth. The midwife, "an artist, a craftswoman," after a successful delivery "gave the war cry which signified that the woman had fought her battle well, that she had been a valiant warrior, that she had taken a captive, that she had captured a child." Tenderly, eloquently, the midwife gave words of joyful welcome, then warning, and finally, comfort to the infant: "O

Preceding pages: Tending the blaze, potters from the village of Atzacualoya, in Guerrero, fire a mound of griddles used for cooking tortillas. Their method varies little from the days of Aztec rule.

PRECEDING PAGES: DAVID HISER
EMBLEM, ABOVE: THE GODDESS TLAZOLTEOTL

precious necklace, O quetzal feather, / O jade, O armlet, O turquoise! . . . / You have come into the world, a place of suffering, a place of affliction, / a place of searing heat, bitter cold, harsh winds. / It is a place of hardship, a place of thirst, a place of hunger. / It is a place of cold, a place of tears. / Indeed, it is not an agreeable place; / it is a place of weeping, a place of sorrow, a place where one suffers affliction. / Here your task shall be weeping, tears, sorrow, fatigue. . . . / Rest now, repose now on this earth. . . ."

To a boy the midwife proclaimed their society's demands: "You are pledged, you are promised, you are sent to the field of battle. / War is your destiny, your calling." She advised a girl: ". . . you shall become worn, you shall become weary. / You are to prepare drink, you are to grind corn, / you are to toil, you are to sweat, beside the ashes, beside the hearth."

If the child died it was buried beside the corn bin for its pure spirit to protect the sustenance of life—"our bones, our flesh." A woman who died in childbirth immediately became deified. Like a warrior killed in battle she went to the "House of the Sun." In her praise the midwife said: "O my little one, my daughter, beloved mistress, / you have wearied yourself, manfully you have fought. / By your labors you have won Our Lord's noble death, glorious death, / truly, now, you have toiled for it, well you merited it; / the good, the fine, the precious death was your recompense, your reward."

Her husband and other mourners protected her body even after burial from warriors who, if the opportunity arose, cut off a middle finger from the corpse as a magic talisman to carry into battle for protection.

Elated kinsmen welcomed each mother's infant with joy, gifts, and feasting. Durán says, "No people on earth have loved their children as the people of this nation do." Soothsayers studied the birth date and predicted good fortune for the child if possible, for each Mexica's fate lay in the cycle of days, whether beneficent or ill-starred. A good day sign and its dominant god could mean a future of glory and riches; an unlucky one could predestine a fate of crime, sloth, and drunkenness. The midwife bathed and purified the newborn child, invoking the water goddess; then she dedicated a boy to the sun's service, and presented him with a small shield and arrows. A girl received miniature spinning and weaving implements.

*C*hildren spent their early years at home under the tutelage of affectionate but firm parents who punished an unruly or idle child by scratching it with maguey thorns or forcing it to breathe the scorching smoke of burning chili peppers. Children learned practical household tasks as early as possible. Boys carried firewood or water. Girls took up the spindle at six. While learning practical skills both constantly heard sage advice from their elders.

In the Mexica love of metaphors these wise words were called "precious jades" or "the box of treasures that our forebears fashioned." In long orations preserved through generations, the young memorized the litany of their duties. In turn, they would someday recite the rigid codes to their own progeny.

As Sahagún recorded and Thelma Sullivan has translated it, noble fathers counseled their sons thus: "You should not give yourself overmuch to sleep lest you are said to be, lest you be called a larva in a cocoon, a slug-abed, a roll of sleep, sleep itself. . . . at night you should arise . . . you should supplicate Our Lord, Lord of All. . . . You should quickly take your broom and sweep, and at the time you awaken, at the time you arise, you must be sure to make an offering of incense. . . . You should be discreet in your manner of walking. . . . lest it be said that you are a simpleton, that you are a vulgar commoner. . . . You should not speak in a high thin voice. . . . Neither should you shout, lest you be regarded as a simpleton, a lunatic, a

A bird receives its plumage from the hands of Fernando Lorenzo, who paints a clay coin bank he hopes to sell at the market in Tepoztlan. In earlier times, cacao beans served as a "coinage" in commerce.

lout, a country bumpkin. . . . When you are called, you should not have to be summoned twice. . . . you should not dress in worn, torn garments. . . . be particularly moderate in food and drink. . . ."

People of lesser rank probably followed this noble ideal of living, and its echoes are heard to this day. Thelma Sullivan told me one man's scathing comment on an inept fellow: "He who does not know how to sweep, does not know how to confess." Unwittingly, this referred to a ritual of sweeping the temple before confessing evil deeds. And in Tepoztlan and other villages custom still prevails: often I awakened at dawn to the sound of a gardener's stiff brush broom sweeping flowered pathways.

Mexica children began to learn such duties while still at home. But at an early age sons and daughters of the nobility left home for a stern and rigid school called *cal-mecac* where they dedicated themselves to Quetzalcoatl, and under the direction of religious leaders endured a strict regimen of learning. When a boy entered the school his father advised, "Listen, my son, you are not going to be honoured, nor obeyed, nor esteemed. You are going to be looked down upon, humiliated, and despised. Every day you will cut agave-thorns for penance, and you will draw blood from your body with these spines. . . ."

Students endured rigorous fasts, labored in the fields and gathered firewood for the temples, suffered severe punishment for the smallest infraction of rules. They never enjoyed a full night's sleep, but rose exhausted at night to journey into the mountains alone. There, they pierced their bodies and let sacrificial blood fall upon the earth. Demanding priests taught them the wisdom of the painted books: songs of the gods; dreams and divination; the reckoning of days and of years. Students also learned "to speak well, to make proper salutations, and to bow." Royal sons came

Fresh from the artist come goods sold at the outdoor market, a fixture in Mexican towns long before the Aztecs. In Tepoztlan, Fernando Lorenzo readies a figure for his collection, which includes ceramic masks and bird-shaped bowls. "I like to tell stories," says Fernán Santos, who touches up a vivid pastoral scene. He paints on paper made from the bark of a fig tree, material on which Aztecs inscribed their pictorial manuscripts.

from other parts of the empire to calmecacs in Tenochtitlan, to be trained as priests and state officials. Well-born girls learned to take part in religious rites and mastered the arts of weaving and needlework taught by priestesses.

The great majority of boys, sons of commoners, attended the less rigid *telpoch-calli* where they studied warfare and dedicated themselves to the powerful and capricious Tezcatlipoca: "the Young Man," "the Warrior," "the Enemy." For noble or commoner, warrior or civilian, Mexica education produced young people thoroughly trained to Mexica ideals of conformity, religion, and war. Soustelle says, "The stoicism with which the Aztecs were able to meet the most terrible ordeals proves that this education attained its end."

In Milpa Alta, a mountain town that was once part of the province of Xochimilco, I noticed men greeting town elders with a low bow and a gesture of kissing their leaders' hands. A young farmer I met had worked in California fields. "I made a lot of money there but I left," he said. "My life is here in Milpa Alta." When I asked him about his formal greeting to older men he replied with a serious nod and a moderate voice, "Yes, it is because there is still much nobleness here."

*T*he formality of long speeches and seemingly endless harangues of "do's and don't's" marked each rite of passage. Girls were warned against the telltale demeanor of a harlot. "She paints her face, variously paints her face; her face is covered with rouge. . . . She perfumes herself. . . . She chews chicle—she clacks chicle. . . . she goes about disgracing the streets, frequenting the market place. . . . Her heart is constantly throbbing; she follows the wide road. . . ." Instead, young noblewomen were urged to seek "goodness, humanity, humaneness, the human way of life, excellence, modesty, the fullness of love."

Spray of water helps Modesta Lavana soften wool she will transform into thread. A nationally recognized weaver, she follows age-old methods in her compound at Hueyapan on the slopes of Popocatepetl. Here women still embrace weaving as an honorable duty. Freshly washed wool from her herd of sheep dries overhead.

Ceremonies graduated young people from the schools and freed them to marry —with still more ceremony. Her hair freshly washed, her face made up, bedecked in red feathers, the bride was borne like a burden on the back of a sturdy woman to the groom's house. As the young couple sat on woven mats, the bridegroom's mantle was tied to the bride's huipil, or blouse. Four older people kneeling at the corners of the couple's small mat advised them on their future life. Relatives and guests had brought gifts, had drunk chocolate and pulque. But there were always rules to be followed. Rituals excepted, only people past middle age might drink enough pulque to become intoxicated; those younger abstained under severe penalties. Noblemen could marry several wives; rulers made numerous dynastic matches, but most men were commoners and married only one wife.

At marriage a man established a household and took up his work, in the specialized occupations of the city or the ancient chores of the land. As an adult he assumed both privileges and duties. He supported his family, paid his taxes, and—as he was taught from birth—went to war for the glory of gods and empire. He and his family served the city until they reached the respite and respect of old age.

"Old men and old women with whitened heads" confessed their sins to Tezcatlipoca and the goddess Tlazolteotl, and did penance, awaiting the hereafter. Those who died by drowning, of dropsy, or were struck by *Continued on page 136*

Weaver's Art

Instructed in weaving as a young girl, as an ancient manuscript records, Modesta Lavana uses the bristly heads of a teasel plant for carding. After hand spinning, she balls the thread, holding a pre-Hispanic spindle whorl between her toes. Before the Spanish brought sheep, weavers fashioned garments out of cotton or maguey fiber.

Patterns lengthen under the skillful hands of Doña Modesta and neighbor Nicolasa Casares as they weave on old-style back-strap looms. Made with undyed yarn (above), the ponchos in progress will require more than a week to complete.

Love of Flowers

Flowers bring together contrasting faces of Mexico on market day in Huauchinango. A vendor offers calla lilies to a shopper who gestures with a handful of tuberoses. At the blessing-of-water ceremony in Huejutla, blossoms provide garlands for a jug of holy water that this girl will carry away. Even in the Aztecs' austere society, people gloried in flowers. They worshiped Xochipilli, the "Prince of Flowers." On this famous statue of him, scholars have recognized natural hallucinogens—a mushroom, a morning glory—that could induce trance or rapture.

MELINDA BERGE

DAVID HISER

132

Warriors of high rank—those who have taken captives unaided in battle—lead a dance with their mistresses to celebrate the feast day of the ninth month, Tlaxochimaco. Known as "the offering of the flowers," this midyear event called for the people of the capital to fill temples and homes with garlands. Their uniforms, jewelry, and plumes proclaiming their status, warriors danced "like a moving serpent" at the main temple to the music of drums and flute. In this feast, and a few others, human sacrifice had no part.

Cult Figures

A day did not pass when the Aztecs, ever anxious about the future, failed to pay homage to their numerous gods. Xiuhtecutli, sculpted to hold objects now lost, received daily offerings of meat and drink. Consecrated women modeled the gods out of the grain amaranth; priests fed them to worshipers. Today, amaranth figures, sold as candy, treat secular heroes like Benito Juárez (right), reformer and President.

lightning, might enjoy perpetual springtime in the paradise of Tlaloc. For others, grieving kinsmen held ceremonies till after four years the spirit's perilous journey to the underworld ended in the timeless dark.

While men served Tezcatlipoca in life, women emulated the great goddess of fourfold nature and many names. Thelma Sullivan has written of this deity and her many roles. As Toci she was "Our Grandmother," as Tonantzin "Our Mother." In other guises she was "Midwife of the Night," "Heart of the Earth." She was the great spinner of the thread and weaver of the fabric of life. Ancient codices depict her wearing a headband of unspun cotton decorated with spindles wound with cotton thread. Fine weaving was particularly the work of the elite, and Sahagún recorded a ruler's advice to his daughter: "Pay heed to, apply yourself to, the work of women. . . . / It is not your destiny, it is not your fate, to offer / [for sale] in people's doorways, / greens, firewood, strings of chiles, slabs of rock salt, / for you are a noblewoman. / [Thus], see to the spindle, the batten. . . ."

On the cloud-dimmed slopes of Popocatepetl women still live by the goddess's ideal. I went there to the village of Hueyapan with young anthropologist Laurencia Alvarez, who has lived there and studied its way of life. She guided me to a woman who chooses the best of ancient and modern worlds and preserves traditional nobleness and skills. Modesta Lavana, known by the respectful title Doña, welcomed us into the high walls of her compound and the confidence of her private universe.

Doña Modesta is a small, sturdy woman whose strong face is framed by dark hair as brilliant as blackbirds' wings in sunlight. That day and on subsequent visits I never saw her stop working.

We fed dried corn shucks to a pen of fat sheep, and I watched as she processed their sheared wool through every step to woven ponchos. As she talked she spun, fashioning fine threads on a spindle. "In Guanajuato in 1978 I won the national wool craft award," she told me. "There, they said as I spun, 'It is impossible! I cannot believe what I am seeing. Your thread is so fine and even.' I answered, 'I am doing what you see, but yes, it is impossible, so close your eyes. It is a dream.' " She laughed delightedly and often; spun; directed the activities of her four daughters and four grandchildren; cooked steaming tortillas, wild greens and mushrooms she had gathered from the volcano's slopes; and in place of rest, she wove. "It takes about two months to soften, card, and spin enough thread for a poncho," she remarked. "Then the weaving takes eight to fifteen days."

Friends came to set up their back-strap looms in the courtyard and spend long afternoons working beside her in pre-Columbian fashion. Nicolasa Casares told me it is a craft learned early. "Some girls start weaving at 12. Others not until they are 15 or even 18. I had no interest in weaving. But when I married, my mother-in-law said, 'You are a wife. You must make a poncho for your husband.' So I separated the wool, carded it, spun thread, and wove one for my husband. That was years ago. I've never stopped. We do it for the family. It is our obligation as women."

Thelma Sullivan points out the ancient symbolism: "spinning and weaving represent life, death, and rebirth in a continuing cycle that characterizes the essential nature of the Mother Goddess." The deity also fostered plant growth and was "goddess of medicines and medicinal plants, and patroness of healers, midwives. . . ."

"I care for the pregnant woman. I bring babies into the world. I heal the sick. I am a curer," Doña Modesta says proudly. "I heal only with the plants that grow from the earth." She bent over herbs and flowers along garden paths to name each one and explain its healing properties in detail. We returned to the courtyard with bundles of leaves and blossoms.

On one visit, Nicolasa had complained of lethargy and often fell asleep at her loom. She had asked to be cured. As she lay on a mat in the courtyard, Doña Modesta massaged her with shredded leaves and flowers. "The body absorbs the juices," she explained as she worked. She pressed Nicolasa's head, the base of her throat, her abdomen. The curer's movements were practiced and assured. Her confident hands massaged, kneaded, clasped, stroked, caressed. "She begins to feel the power," she said finally, and bound a poultice of vinegar-soaked herbs to her patient's abdomen. To "cleanse" Nicolasa's body, Doña Modesta rubbed it gently with a fresh uncracked egg, then "cooled" it with gentle sweeps from a bundle of leaves. "When your blood is 'hot' you feel dizzy, nervous. With this it is cured, the body is balanced," she said.

*T*lazolteotl was "Grandmother of the Bathhouse . . . the warm, moist womb of the Mother Goddess."

"I use my bathhouse here in the compound for curing with heat and herbs," Doña Modesta said, pointing to a large, rounded adobe structure. "But I am building one far from here where the plants grow wild. That is better. To go to nature, to the countryside as a place to heal. But I do not always use herbs to make someone whole again."

The goddess was "Eater of Ordure," deeply revered. "Transgressors confessed their iniquities to her . . . such as murder and adultery, which she ingested, and by so doing, unraveled, so to speak, the fabric of evil the penitent had woven." After confession an Aztec "was like the thread on the spindle ready to be woven anew."

"I work with the doctor here," Doña Modesta says. "We are friends, and I give injections if someone brings the medicine from him. But these medicines only get rid of pain. They don't cure the real illness. I cure the body with herbs, but I also cure the heart. If people are full of hate and fighting or if a married couple is unhappy they come to me. This unhappiness is an illness. I talk to them, calm them, get them to talk to me and then to each other. They leave here healed and complete again."

The great goddess was "Our Mother," "Our Grandmother," "Heart of the Earth."

Doña Modesta's kitchen is a separate small building in the center of the compound. It serves as the hub of family life. I have spent many pleasant hours there chatting or sipping a sweet, hot drink of corn, water, and chocolate, a modern blend of ancient ingredients. Her younger daughters cook on a modern stove in the main house; but she prefers the pre-Columbian hearth of three stones or a larger one made of adobe bricks plastered with a mixture of ashes and the residue water of lime-soaked corn—"because in every part these hearths are made of nature."

*E*ach generation in her family speaks Spanish, but she insists they also speak Nahuatl—"It is our true language." Even toddlers are well-mannered and well-spoken. If not, she rebukes them kindly, but firmly. "It is the way I was raised," she told me. "My father said, 'I am raising sons and daughters, not a herd of animals.' We behaved in the way he expected."

In her darkened kitchen late one afternoon, fire played shadows across her strong face. As she spun she said, "I am skilled at medicine, but yet I failed. Not long ago I held my sick daughter in my arms. I could do nothing more. I said to her, 'I gave you life, nurtured you. I can cure others, why can I not help you, my own child?' She left a little son. I have taken him as my own and changed his name to Gregorio, my father's name. He has duties. At dawn he sweeps the compound, he feeds the rabbits we raise. He does well at school—third grade already."

The afternoon grew late. Thunder cracked and echoed through ravines in the volcano's slopes as torrents of tropical rain fell outside. She hugged a frightened granddaughter and calmed the toddler with a kiss. "This is where I like to be—in my kitchen," she said. "I am content. Often I spread a straw mat here to sleep on the dirt floor beside the fire. Then all night I am between my family in the house and my animals in their pens. I am in the center." She turned her large, dark eyes to mine. "I gain strength from lying next to the earth."

It was my final visit to Doña Modesta and Hueyapan. We said farewell. As the muddy road curved away and steeply downward, I looked back, but the village had disappeared. A dark and heavy cloud enclosed it and bound it to the verdant, fertile slope of the volcano.

Centuries ago when the Mexica captured towns like Hueyapan, their warriors might expect to gain farmland as a reward for great exploits. By then their officers were specialists, men of the obsidian-edged wooden sword who never used the digging stick themselves. And if they took citizens of Hueyapan to Tenochtitlan to be slaves, that consigned them to the lowest rank of society.

A slave was not a citizen, not paid by his owner. A master, however, was responsible for housing, clothing, and feeding slaves as if they were citizens, and theirs was not a life without hope. Only the incorrigible would be sacrificed. Although slavery was the punishment for various crimes, people might sell themselves to settle a debt or to assure a livelihood. Slaves might become managers of estates, and command free men. A slave might regain freedom when a relative took his place, when he earned money for his owner, or when the owner died. One about to be sold became free if he escaped to the palace and the presence of the ruler. Moreover, the children of slaves came into the world as free—Itzcoatl the most famous example.

Ownership could be as precarious as it was desirable. Masters dared not mistreat slaves, for they were Tezcatlipoca's "well-beloved children." According to Sahagún, if "a slave freed himself and grew rich, and . . . the slave-owner became in his turn a

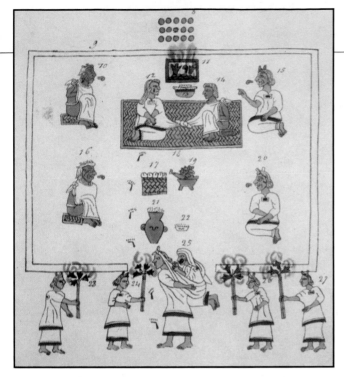

"Do not weary of the load called marriage," elders advise at an Aztec wedding. Taken from the Codex Mendoza, a drawing describes the nuptial ceremony. This begins when a vigorous woman, surrounded by female relatives bearing torches, carries the bride into the bridegroom's house. After the elderly witnesses deliver lengthy and eloquent counsel, a solemn knotting of the couple's garments together symbolizes their union. The custom persists to this day in Mexican villages.

slave, it was said that this was the will of Tezcatlipoca, who had heard the slave's prayer and had had pity on him, and had punished the master for his hardness to his servants."

Free people without land, called *tlalmaitl,* or "hand of the earth," may have been people uprooted by war or civil turmoil. They labored for landowners and paid rent by a form of share-cropping.

*T*he great majority of Mexica were the *macehualtin,* the workers. These were the free commoners, the thousands of citizens who formed the labor force of Tenochtitlan. A *macehualli* had a humble house of his own on land owned by his family. When necessary he performed communal tasks—cleaning and maintaining buildings, roads, and bridges—or fought for the state. In return he had his rights to justice as defined by law, a public school for his children, and perhaps a modest share in the distribution of tribute. He belonged to the barefoot masses who dressed in a simple loincloth and short mantle, or a plain knee-length overblouse and skirt of coarse fabric. These were the folk who grew food for the city, transported it across the broad lakes, and sold a few vegetables, baskets, or other simple wares in the markets.

Most who were born commoners died commoners, but humble individuals might rise to higher status by courage, intelligence, and hard work. "Birth played its part," concludes Soustelle, "but it was still personal merit that raised a man, and lack of it that lowered him."

Once when Moctezuma II picked an ear of corn without permission, the farmer reprimanded him for his illegal deed. The emperor offered to return the corn, and the farmer refused to accept it. Then, Soustelle says, Moctezuma "gave him his own cloak . . . and said to his dignitaries, 'This poor man has shown more courage than anybody here, for he has dared to reproach me to my face with having broken my own laws.' And he raised the peasant to the rank of tecuhtli, entrusting him with the government of Xochimilco.'"

Valor in battle, especially, could win status, riches, and glory for a commoner.

Even a schoolboy yearning for battle, according to Durán, might be "sent to carry food and other supplies to the warriors so that he might see action and hardship . . . if he showed bravery on the battlefield, he was soon admitted to the company of warriors. Consequently, he often went to the field with his load and returned a captain, bearing the insignia of a valorous man." Heroes who captured as many as four prisoners rose dramatically in status, and the emperor conferred much-coveted honors on them: elegant capes that reached below the knee, jewels prescribed for the rank.

The artisans who fashioned luxury items seemed to be in a class apart. Very likely some originally came from other areas of the empire, for they lived in their own neighborhoods, associated with each other socially and professionally in guilds, held to their own customs, elected leaders from their ranks, and raised their children in the tradition of their own skills. These were the painters, featherworkers, smiths of gold and silver, and lapidaries so skilled they were called the *tolteca*. They did not amass great wealth or power, but held an esteemed position in society.

After seeing Aztec treasures at court in Spain, the diplomat Peter Martyr wrote: "If ever artists of this kind of work have touched genius, then surely these natives are they. It is not so much the gold or the precious stones I admire, as the cleverness of the artist and the workmanship, which much exceed the value of the material and excite my amazement." He describes a

---

A sacred book—the Codex Borbonicus— yields the intricacies of the Aztec calendar to students at a calmecac, *a school where priests instructed children of the noble class. A strict code of behavior called for regular bloodletting. Students also hauled firewood and swept floors. Sons of commoners attended less severe schools that made them into warriors.*

necklace "formed by four circles of little golden chains, ornamented with two hundred red stones and one hundred and seventy two green stones; ten large precious stones set in gold, from which are suspended one hundred and fifty admirably wrought pendants, hang from this collar." He adds, "I am at a loss to describe the aigrettes, the plumes, and the feather fans."

These plumes, each a "Shadow of the gods," arrived in tribute or trade with other raw materials. After the tolteca fashioned them into works of art worthy of an emperor—whether Aztec or Spanish—the pochteca packed for trade those treasures not reserved for the local elite.

By the time Moctezuma II became emperor, the traders had risen dramatically in wealth and, naturally, in importance. While his courts judged all other citizens, these entrepreneurs had judges of their own who settled their cases and even had the power of death over offenders. The pochteca lived in their own neighborhoods, reared their children to succeed them, and worshiped their own gods in their own temples with distinctive ceremonies. They devoted their lives to private gain, but vehemently denied riches, walking about the city in patched and tattered mantles, swearing with downcast eyes they sought neither fame nor honor. This ostentatious humility was a form of self-defense, for each trader knew that boastfulness would offend his superiors—traders did not enter the ruling class by virtue of their wealth. Among themselves the merchants competed fiercely for eminence.

From a hard-pressed tribe with poverty and danger the common lot, the Mexica had become a triumphant nation—with many still poor, some on the rise, a few making a show of splendor. Strain between the haves and have-nots must have fed the anxiety that haunted the city. Ahuitzotl had welcomed the valiant pochteca at

court; his successor preferred rigid divisions of rank.

The highest officials were *tecutli*, or lords. These were the generals, city or regional governors, and senior judges. A tecutli dressed elegantly, lived in a palace, and held land tended by peasants. He paid no taxes. Many gained their office by appointment from the emperor; none could select a son to inherit the position. Like rulership it passed to the most qualified person, usually in the family but not always.

Neighborhood chiefs in the capital, and the elders who advised them, composed a lesser rank who kept district records and census reports up to date. Civil servants recorded the activities of each household, noting taxes, public works, and military service. Durán says simply that the officials of the realm were so numerous that no one could possibly count them.

Similarly, priests descended in rank from the highest order to those of lesser responsibilities.

*N*o matter what the rank or office in Tenochtitlan, the tlatoani ruled over all. Although bound to respect sacred custom, he was sovereign in religion and government. He was Tezcatlipoca's surrogate on earth, his voice, his action: "he speaks within you, he makes you his lips, his jaws, his ears. . . . He also makes you his fangs, his claws, for you are his wild beast, you are his eater-of-people, you are his judge."

The emperor was a mighty tree that spread its wide branches to protect the people. Rulership was a heavy burden to be borne as a dutiful slave bent to the task of a heavy load. The monarch was "the mother, the father of the city." Princely preparation for the royal life was never taken lightly. The ruler told his sons of their all-inclusive responsibilities. "See to the dancing and singing with drum and rattle in order to arouse the city and give pleasure to the Lord of All, the Supreme Lord. . . .

The Natural Way

Her garden serving as pharmacy, Doña Modesta administers a native remedy to Nicolasa Casares to rid her of lethargy. One of several curers in Hueyapan, Doña Modesta first massaged her patient with shredded plants and flowers, including floripondio, *(lower left), so "the body absorbs the juices." Now she applies a poultice of vinegar-soaked herbs to the abdomen and finishes by rubbing the body with an egg. In her garden grows the Aztec lily (upper left), used by healers to reduce fever. These folk cures likely will not die out—two granddaughters, who observe the procedure, later mimicked it in play.*

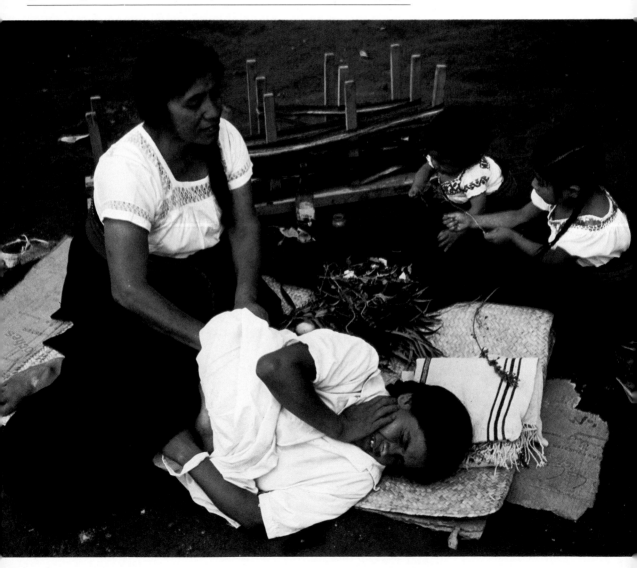

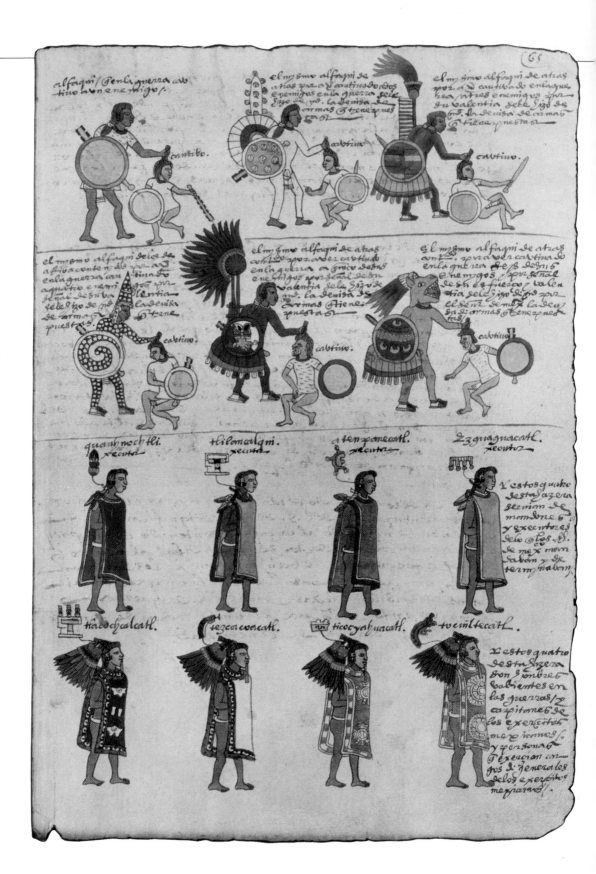

alfaqui/ senla guerra cabtino avn enemigo/

el mismo alfaqui de atras por aver cabtivado dos enemigos enla guerra sele dio yd la denisa d'armas o tenezones

el mismo alfaqui de atras por aver cabtivado enla guerra/ a tres enemigos por su valentia sele dio de gñ la denisa de armas o titica y nesta

cabtibo.

cabtino.

cabtiuo.

el mismo alfaqui delos de atras a conten ido por aver enla guerra/ avn cabtino a quatro enemigos por su valentia sele dio de gñ de armas puestas.

el mismo alfaqui de atras cobido por aver cabtivado enla guerra a cinco de sus enemigos por señal de su valentia dela qual yd la denisa d'armas o tiene ynesta

El mismo alfaqui de atras cobido por aver cabtivado enla guerra de seis de sus enemigos por señal de su esfuerzo y valentia sele dio d'gñ por el sene seme y la denisa d's armas o tenezo nestas

cabtino.

cabtino.

cabtino.

quauhnochtli. tecutli

tlilancalqui. tecutli

atenpanecatl. tecutli

ezquaguacatl. tecutli

Y estos quatro destaçera del mismo mombre y exentores delos. cõ. de mex moro sabon y d'termi nabom/

tlatochcalcatl.

tezcacoacatl.

ticocyahuacatl.

tocuiltecatl.

Y estos quatro destaçera son jonbres sabientes en las guerras/ y capitanes d' los exercitos mexicomos/ y personas. Y execian co gos d' jenerales d'lo exercitos mexianos/

See to the arts, to the featherwork art. . . . And particularly give your attention to the cultivation of the land. . . . Nowhere have I seen that one has breakfasted and dined on nobility. . . . And where have I seen someone without provisions effect a conquest? . . . put yourselves close to, by the side of Our Lord. . . . Will it be you, the eldest? Will it be you, the second son? Or will it be you, the youngest who perhaps shall be the clear-witted one?"

Moctezuma II was not the eldest son, but the one most qualified in the eyes of his peers. Six decades after the investiture of his great-grandfather Moctezuma I, on the same ritual day, he was dressed in the royal raiment and crowned with the turquoise diadem. Already he had acted as a priest of Huitzilopochtli, a heroic general whose army had captured 5,100 prisoners for sacrifice at his coronation ceremony. Now in assuming the burden of his distinguished royal dynasty he went further than his predecessors and proclaimed himself sacrosanct—semi-divine.

Thelma Sullivan says, "The ruler may have been regarded as the mother and father of the people, the great cypress, the great silk-cotton tree under which they could seek protection, but on occasion he became a wild beast; he bared his fangs and showed his claws. He was, in short, a despot." It was said that to be in his presence was "to be in a place full of scorpions, to be in a place full of nettles."

As the earthly representative of the most powerful deity, Moctezuma declared

his palace a "House of God." He discharged all officials appointed by Ahuitzotl because "many of them were of low descent." Only nobles of legitimate birth attended him. Even his half brothers did not qualify—he believed they showed characteristics of their non-royal mothers. "Because, just as precious stones appear out of place among poor and wretched ones, so those of royal blood seem ill-assorted among people of low extraction."

Visiting lords approached him reverently, unshod, humbly dressed. He wore only the richest of clothing, and his gold-sandaled feet did not walk on unswept ground. The rooms of his palace numbered into the hundreds, his palace staff into the thousands. Bernal Díaz said, "His cooks prepared over thirty kinds of dishes for every meal . . . He was served on a very low table, on which they spread white cloths and large napkins . . . He drank cacao from cups of fine gold."

Durán comments on the perfect behavior expected from the nobles: "If Moteczoma heard any complaints against their comportment, he would have them pierced with arrows or burned alive." They did not gaze directly into their ruler's eyes, and all prostrated themselves at his approach. Any commoner who dared even to glance at him was put to death. When Durán questioned an Indian about the emperor's appearance he heard the astonishing reply, "Father, I will not lie to you or tell you about things which I do not know. I never saw his face!"

This severe human-god held the seat of all power, but he also was the center of cosmic responsibility. In the cycle of days, months, seasons, and years the Mexica and their deities had become locked into a morbid cycle of mutual support. Without the gods' favors humanity would disappear. Without blood ritual, which had increased with every ruler, the deities would perish.

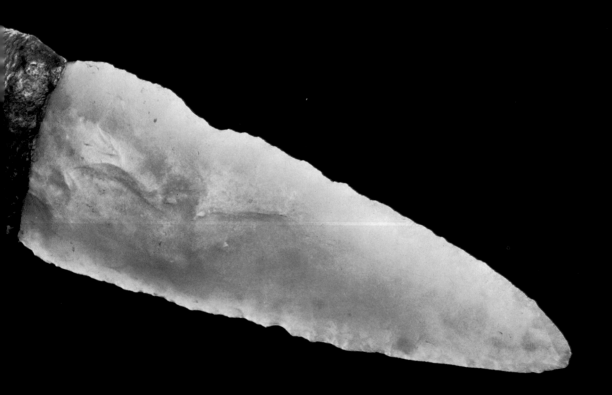

A Duty to Feed the Gods

Life flowed from death—so believed the Aztecs, who
practiced human sacrifice on a scale unprecedented in
Mesoamerica. Blood nourished the deities and thus
sustained the world. The mosaic image of an eagle
knight marks this stone knife as reserved for rites of
the sun: A priest cut out the living heart, as depicted in
the Florentine Codex. As the empire grew, only
blood and more blood upheld its fragile confidence.

No one dared deny what the gods demanded in a world they knew was doomed from the day of its creation. That day had begun the age of *ollin*—movement. With "movement" it would end. Anyone who survived the cataclysmic final earthquake faced certain death at the hands of the monsters of the twilight who lurked within the skies. But there were other dangers.

The aging Nezahualpilli warned Moctezuma, "I have discovered that in a very few years our cities will be ravaged and destroyed. We and our children will be killed. . . . before many days have passed you will see signs in the sky. . . ." In 1510 a holy servant of Huitzilopochtli saw "a marvelous and terrifying comet" rise into the eastern sky. Moctezuma summoned his soothsayers to interpret its meaning. They replied they had not seen it. Enraged, he had them imprisoned. Nezahualpilli assured him the omen foretold disaster and declared that death "will dominate the land!"

The emperor wept bitterly, moaning to Nezahualpilli, "Why should I be the one . . . ? What shall I do? Where shall I hide? Where shall I conceal myself? Alas, if only I could turn into stone, wood, or some other earthly matter rather than suffer that which I so dread!" Further omens and portents continued to beset Moctezuma. Anxiously he ordered old men and women of the city to recount dreams of fate. A man had dreamed of Huitzilopochtli's temple falling in flames, women of a raging river destroying the palace. Moctezuma had the trusting dreamers jailed and fed "in small measures until they starved to death." Yet a noblewoman four days dead rose from the grave to tell him, "in thy time the city of Mexico will end." Misshapen people with two heads and one body walked through the city, then disappeared. A strange ash-gray bird with a mirror on its head was brought to him. The mirror showed him the heavens and stars, then "a number of people, coming massed, coming as conquerors, coming in war panoply." Fire consumed a temple of Huitzilopochtli, and lightning struck another. On a clear, calm day waves of uncanny size and force churned in the lake, drowning people and destroying houses.

Nezahualpilli had died during these years of crisis, leaving Moctezuma to witness the omens without that monarch's seasoned advice. The panic-stricken people of Tenochtitlan heard voices in the night. A ghostly woman wailed loudly, "My children, we must flee far away from this city." At times she cried, "My children, where shall I take you?"

And Tezcatlipoca mocked his people once again. The terrified Mexica lay in their darkened houses and listened as The Lord of the Night, The Enemy, played his flute through the silent streets of the city. The desperate king thought of fleeing to a cave for refuge with Huemac, last lord of Tula, now a Lord of the Dead.

Yet he stayed, did penance, prayed, performed private rituals to the Morning Star. Nezahualpilli had warned him of it. At certain positions it portended evil; on a given day it would bring menace upon the emperor. It was Quetzalcoatl revealed. The star rose, vanished, appeared as the Evening Star, disappeared and rose again in a steady rhythm like a shuttle on a loom. Moctezuma, the mother and father of his people, watched as it played back and forth across the heavens, weaving the fabric of certain doom across the Mexica universe.

"Aztec ideal of beauty": Curator Felipe Solís thus describes a temple statue that held a jade heart. It represents "the perfect citizen in maturity—one who, through life or death, sought only glory for his state."

THE STRANGERS

"Broken spears lie in the roads; we have torn our hair in our grief. The houses are roofless now, and their walls are red with blood."

The crippled man was a common man and loyal, who came from the Forest of the Afterworld near the Gulf Coast. There he had seen a miracle so inexplicable he walked all the way to the highlands and on to the capital city in spite of the fact he had no toes. He told Moctezuma he had watched "a mountain range or small mountain floating in the midst of the water, and moving here and there without touching the shore. My lord, we have never seen the like of this, although we guard the coast and are always on watch."

Nor had Moctezuma heard the like of it; he found this the most incredible of all the omens. He sent envoys hurrying to verify the news. Durán says two of them climbed a tree and saw "in the middle of the water a house from which appeared white men, their faces white and their hands likewise.

Preceding pages: Day's fading light betokens the end of the Aztec Empire. Here, on the Gulf of Mexico, Cortés destroyed his ships; now his men would follow him inland—to conquest or death.
EMBLEM, ABOVE: QUETZALCOATL AS THE WIND GOD

They have long thick beards and their clothing is of all colors. . . ."

Hearing this, Moctezuma "lowered his head and, without answering a word, placed his hand upon his mouth. In this way he remained for a long time." Of course the dumbfounded emperor knew nothing of Spaniards. But it was a year One Reed, an anniversary of Quetzalcoatl's birth and a suitable year for his return. Now his subjects marveled at the mysterious shapes that prowled along the shores.

Hernán Cortés was exploring the coast in 1519, searching for members of a previous expedition, dropping anchor from time to time to trade with the Indian inhabitants. In April he went ashore within the bounds of the Aztec Empire. With a hundred sailors, his 11 ships carried 508 men—some of them black—16 horses, and a few cannon. In addition, he brought a shipwrecked Spaniard rescued in Yucatan who had learned a Maya language, and an Indian woman remembered as Doña Marina or La Malinche who spoke both Maya and Nahuatl. By three-stage translations Cortés could communicate with speakers of Nahuatl. Doña Marina advised Cortés shrewdly and aided him greatly.

News of Cortés's arrival threw Moctezuma into extreme distress. He ordered the best goldsmiths, lapidaries, and featherworkers to fashion gifts for these beings. Nervously recalling dreadful omens and old traditions, he ordered the strangers received with propriety befitting gods—but he also sent messages he hoped would delay them. He said to his messengers: "According to the legends, they are to acquire all the wealth that we now possess. If it is really Quetzalcoatl, greet him on my behalf and give him these gifts. . . . I have always considered that my domain was only lent to me. Let him permit me to end my days here. Then let him return to enjoy what is his!"

Led by one of the realm's greatest lords, the envoys rushed to the coast with the new gifts and also the sacred attire of the gods Quetzalcoatl, Tezcatlipoca, and Tlaloc. On shipboard the Mexica prostrated themselves before Cortés; then he allowed them to dress him as Quetzalcoatl. "With great care they fastened the turquoise mask in place, the mask of the god with its crossband of quetzal feathers," a collar with a golden disk, and a cloak. "In his hand they placed the shield with its fringe and pendant of quetzal feathers, its ornaments of gold and mother-of-pearl." They spread the other regalia before him. Cortés asked calmly, "And is this all? Is this your gift of welcome?"

He gave the emissaries glass beads, trinkets, and food, then caused them to faint with a demonstration of cannon fire and revived them with wine "so good and easy to swallow that they had lost their senses with it." Allowed to leave, they raced back to Moctezuma, who thought "they had seen the gods, their eyes had looked on their faces."

Moctezuma grew terrified as he heard of the cannon. "A thing like a ball of stone comes out of its entrails: it comes out shooting sparks and raining fire. The smoke that comes out with it has a pestilent odor, like that of rotten mud. . . . If the cannon is aimed against a mountain, the mountain splits and cracks open."

Food of the strangers was "large and white. . . . something like straw, but with the taste of a cornstalk, of the pith of a cornstalk." The envoys presented Spanish hardtack to the emperor, and he noted that the food of the gods weighed more than a chunk of tufa stone. He ordered the biscuit taken to Tula and buried in the temple of Quetzalcoatl. Priests reverently "placed it in a gilded gourd, wrapped the latter in rich mantles and made a long procession. . . . He gave orders that the necklace be buried at the feet of the god Huitzilopochtli . . . in the midst of the burning of

The Warnings

In fear and awe, Moctezuma II stands on his palace roof as a comet cleaves the sky, one of eight portents that deeply unnerved him. A decade later, an Indian hiding in a tree observes a Spanish ship off the coast. Descriptions of the vessel as a "mountain that moved" appalled the Aztec monarch.

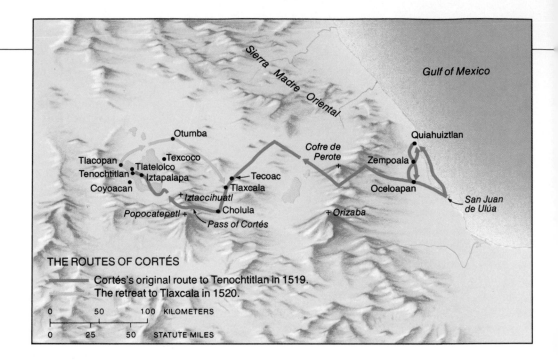

Sierra Madre Oriental

Gulf of Mexico

Otumba

Quiahuiztlan

Tlacopan
Texcoco
Tlatelolco
Tenochtitlan • Iztapalapa
Coyoacan

Cofre de
Perote
+

Zempoala

Tecoac
Tlaxcala
+ Iztaccihuatl

Oceloapan

Popocatepetl +
Cholula
Pass of Cortés

+ Orizaba

San Juan
de Ulúa

THE ROUTES OF CORTÉS

Cortés's original route to Tenochtitlan in 1519.
The retreat to Tlaxcala in 1520.

0   50   100   KILOMETERS

0   25   50   STATUTE MILES

The Route to Tenochtitlan

On his route to conquest, as traced by anthropologist S. Jeffrey K. Wilkerson (map), Cortés recruited allies weary of Aztec overlordship. At Zempoala, he enlisted the Totonac Indians—disaffected, tribute-paying subjects of Moctezuma II. At right, the author and her party, who journeyed with Dr. Wilkerson along the trail of the conquerors, visit Zempoala's main temple-pyramid; a smaller temple stands in a field of drying corn (left). While in Totonac territory, Cortés ordered the capture of five Aztec tax collectors; later he let two of them escape with a message to Moctezuma telling of the high regard in which the Spaniards held him. This stratagem committed the Totonacs to an alliance with Cortés, while forestalling hostile reaction by the Aztec emperor.

incense, the sounding of conch shells and other instruments."

Of the dogs, the emperor heard they were "enormous, with flat ears and long, dangling tongues. The color of their eyes is a burning yellow; their eyes flash fire and shoot off sparks. . . ." They were said to be spotted like jaguars. "When Motecuhzoma heard this report, he was filled with terror. It was as if his heart had fainted, as if it had shriveled. It was as if he were conquered by despair."

While the monarch wavered between panic and inertia, Cortés moved toward a decision. At the Totonac city of Zempoala, which Bernal Díaz called "the city of abundance," he discovered a situation he could turn to his advantage. All was not well in the mighty Aztec Empire.

Local Totonacs hated their distant masters. The Fat Chief made the strangers welcome with vehement complaints about his servitude. At nearby Quiahuiztlan, the Spaniards saw the unexpected arrival of Mexica tax collectors so arrogant they came armed with nothing more than bouquets of flowers: "Each one was smelling the roses he carried. . . ." Although the Totonac chiefs paled in the Mexica presence, Cortés persuaded them to imprison the officials. In a surge of confidence, the Fat Chief allied himself with Cortés.

Cortés was as shocked by Totonac religion as he was pleased with the generosity

Children romp in Zempoala, where Cortés may first have witnessed the ritual taking of human life. One of his men, Bernal Díaz, wrote that "every day they sacrificed . . . three, four, or five Indians," and offered their hearts to their idols. The Spaniards broke the idols and cast them out, had the main temple cleansed and refurbished, and put in their place a cross and an image of the Virgin Mary.

*Daunting ridges and sinuous valleys of the Sierra Madre
Oriental dominate the terrain Cortés and his Indian allies
crossed on their march westward to Tenochtitlan. A ridgetop
trail suggests why the Aztecs called a road* coatl, *or serpent:
a winding course, and the risk of death.*

Trails of Empire

In a grass-grown field, Dr. Wilkerson surveys the ruined temple of the Wind God at Oceloapan. "I am quite sure this was the first inland village Cortés visited, one he found hastily abandoned by Totonacs fearful of the fair-skinned strangers," he says. He and the author's party travel over an ancient paved road, much like those that led the eager but wary Spaniards to Tenochtitlan.

of his new friends. Black-robed priests, their hair matted stiff with human blood, served images that the Spaniards found loathsome. Bernal Díaz says, "every day they sacrificed before our eyes three, four, or five Indians, whose hearts were offered to those idols and whose blood was plastered on the walls." Cortés demanded a stop to this, and promised a deeper friendship in return. Much distressed, the fat dignitary pleaded, "Our angered gods will send locusts to devour our harvests, hail to wreck them, drought to burn them, and torrential rain to swamp them. . . ."

After a tense dispute, says Bernal Díaz, "some fifty of us soldiers clambered up and overturned the idols, which rolled down the steps and were smashed to pieces." The Spaniards made four priests cut their hair and don white robes to tend an image of the Virgin Mary installed in the temple—to sweep, and bring flowers.

During a bountiful Totonac harvest, I sat with Jeff Wilkerson in front of that empty temple, at the top of steps that had echoed the crash of falling gods. As we reread Díaz's account of Spanish-Totonac alliance and conflict, children played on the platform in the plaza below. There, perhaps for the first time, Cortés saw priests offer pulsating hearts to the gods.

"I believe Cortés made his decision to march to Tenochtitlan here," said Jeff. "Until Zempoala he was an explorer." Assured of Totonac support, Cortés strengthened a fortified base called Villa Rica de la Vera Cruz, punished dissenters in his party, sent one ship home and destroyed the rest. As he told his king, "On this all abandoned any hope of leaving. . . ."

Brooding over the reports from the coast, Moctezuma summoned his most expert magicians. Sahagún says he ordered them to bewitch the Spaniards: "to direct a harmful wind against them, or cause them to break out in sores, or. . . . repeat some

Tlaxcalan warrior allies lead an assault against Aztec forces that include a jaguar knight. Aztec reinforcements arrive by canoe as a brigantine brings Cortés and Doña Marina (top) to a causeway to Tenochtitlan, near a shrine to the goddess Toci. This took place late in the conquest.

enchanted word, over and over, that would cause them to fall sick, or die, or return to their own land." Their mission failed, and Moctezuma "did nothing but wait. He did nothing but resign himself and wait for them to come. He mastered his heart at last, and waited for whatever was to happen."

In mid-August Cortés began his march toward Tenochtitlan with 200 Totonac porters and 40 fighting chiefs to aid him and guide his army to the Tlaxcalans, stubborn warriors who had never submitted to the Triple Alliance. Jeff, Mark, Ann, and I were to glimpse the hardships of such a journey.

"I'll take you to a Totonac town that belonged to the Aztecs," Jeff said. "We can go to one by car on a good paved road, or another at the end of a dirt road by second-class bus. Then there's one in the sierra on a very old trail. It's still very pre-Columbian and colonial, but that can be a dangerous journey—bandits!" A few days later, Mark and Ann sat astride mules padded with burlap sacks as Jeff hauled me up into a 16th-century-style wooden saddle to begin my first horseback ride.

For hours we climbed. A wide meadow gave onto stone trails so steep that at times they were laid like stairs. On our journey up to Xochitlan and our return, horses slipped or fell on stones old at the Spanish conquest, improved and worn smooth again in colonial times. Pack mules dawdled, bucked, brayed, kicked; volatile muleteers screamed insults concerning the indifferent animals' lineage. My little mare shivered beneath me near the steepest grades and most precipitous drops.

teçiquauhtitlã

As officials in ancient times would have greeted pochteca or tax collectors, the town council sat assembled to greet us with formality. The two-room schoolhouse became guest quarters. On market day we mingled with the Totonac crowd as they bought a variety of goods from chili peppers to textiles, two of the items once paid as tribute to Tenochtitlan. Jeff cautioned us again as we left: "Travelers are robbed—even killed—on these trails." Descending slowly in the rain, we took comfort when we met a patrol of armed soldiers.

Once the Spanish troops had struggled through the sierra, they approached Tlaxcalan country and hoped to find allies; but past a border fortress, near the town of Tecoac, they met a hostile army "large enough to eclipse the sun." In this, a pitched battle, the small group of Spaniards fought "men as numerous as the sands of the sea. . . . many Spaniards shed

tears and wished that they had not been born, cursing Cortés for having brought them to this fearful end." Encircled and attacked repeatedly—despite their horsemen and artillery—the Spaniards held their ground. They had learned that the Indians' stone-edged wooden swords "cut worse than a knife" and the darts could pierce "any armour." Word spread about that the gods possessed "fiery lightning and with each shot many men perished. . . ."

The staunch Tlaxcalans attacked the Spaniards, then welcomed them as allies. Tlaxcalans hated their neighbors at Cholula, people currently allied with the Mexica—a nation even more despised. Thousands of Tlaxcala's seasoned warriors eagerly joined the Spanish advance.

Cortés held an advantage not only in weapons and tactics, but in psychology as well. Indian terror of the strangers and their animals had spread. Messengers had

Looming above sunlit clouds, the sacred volcano
Popocatepetl echoes the shadowed slope of the
great pyramid of Cholula, topped by the Church
of Our Lady of the Remedies. Pre-Columbian
art historian Richard Townsend describes such holy
mountains as "great natural icons." Cortés
fought at Cholula and later trod the volcano's flank.

reported black men with odd hair, men with skin so white it might have been lime. "They dress in iron and wear iron casques on their heads. Their swords are iron; their bows are iron; their shields are iron; their spears are iron. Their deer carry them on their backs wherever they wish to go."

Indians who saw the "deer" said they were tall as houses: "They make a loud noise when they run; they make a great din, as if stones were raining on earth. . . . It opens wherever their hooves touch it." On the coast and in Tlaxcala those who dared approach the monsters offered them meat, tortillas, and turkeys before discovering they ate grass, grain, and fodder.

Now, hoping to win Cortés away from the Tlaxcalans, Moctezuma urged him to come to Tenochtitlan. But from Cholula, the terror increased. Cholula was a great center of the cult of Quetzalcoatl. When throngs assembled in the temple courtyard, Spaniards and Tlaxcalans blocked every exit. "Then the sudden slaughter began: knife strokes, and sword strokes, and death." Thousands died. Tenochtitlan lay just beyond the volcanoes. When news of the massacre reached the city, the common people "could do nothing but tremble with fright. It was as if the earth trembled beneath them, or as if the world were spinning before their eyes. . . ."

Once more the Spaniards marched: "a multitude," wrote Sahagún, "raising a great dust. . . . the shimmer of their swords was as of a sinuous water course. . . . Some came completely encased in iron—as if turned to iron, gleaming, resounding from afar. And ahead of them, preceding them, ran their dogs, panting, with foam continually dripping from their muzzles."

After the army crossed the snow-whitened pass, Moctezuma's emissaries met them with gifts: streamers of quetzal plumes—and gold, streamers and necklaces of gold. The Mexica looked on amazed at the Spaniards' reaction: "They seized upon the gold as if they were monkeys. . . .

In Doña Modesta's traditional kitchen at Hueyapan, her daughter Irene works dough on a stone metate (left); a tortilla cooks on a clay griddle set on the wood-burning adobe-and-plaster hearth. Pottery dishes by the fire hold servings of boiled and candied squash.

clearly their thirst for gold was insatiable; they starved for it; they lusted for it; they wanted to stuff themselves with it as if they were pigs."

Once more Moctezuma's magicians and sorcerers tried to halt the fateful advance. Near the volcanoes they met a man who appeared to be drunk. His voice of harsh reproof came as if from far away. "Why have you come here? It is useless. . . . Go back, go back! Turn your eyes toward the city. What was fated to happen has already taken place!"

Staring, they saw the whole city in flames, "as if a great battle were raging. . . . This was not a mere mortal. This was the young Tezcatlipoca!" And he disappeared before their eyes. Aghast, they rushed back to Tenochtitlan.

Cortés's forces approached the city on November 8, 1519. Far larger than any city in Spain, it lay before them, enormous, glistening above its vast sparkling lake.

Elated and apprehensive, they stepped onto one of the causeways. Meanwhile, says Sahagún, "Mexico lay as if stunned, silent. None went out of doors. Mothers kept their children in. The roads were clear—wide open, deserted, as if it were early morning."

In full royal state, the lords of the Triple Alliance met Cortés on the causeway. Bernal Díaz saw the great Moctezuma descend from his fine litter to stand under a sumptuous canopy of green plumes, gold, silver, pearls, and green stones. "He was richly dressed"—precious stones adorned the straps of his sandals, which had soles of gold. Four great lords supported him; noblemen and princes swept the way before him and spread mats "so that he would not have to walk on the ground."

Cortés dismounted to bow to the emperor, wish him health, and present a perfumed necklace of glass beads on a golden cord. He "was going to embrace" the Lord of Mexico, but princes caught his arm, "for they thought it an indignity."

Sahagún recorded Moctezuma's greeting to the "god": "You have arrived at your city, Mexico. Here you have come to sit upon your throne and seat. . . . The lords and kings Itzcóatl, the elder Moctezuma, Axayácatl, Tízoc, Ahuítzotl. Oh, for what a short time they protected and guarded the city of Mexico on your behalf. . . . No, I am not dreaming, nor am I rising heavy with sleep. I am not seeing in dreams, nor seeing visions.

"I have in truth seen you and have now set eyes upon your face. . . . take possession of your royal abodes. . . . Come to your land, O lords."

A chronicle tells that Moctezuma arrayed his guests with diadems and necklaces and garlands of flowers, and then with necklaces of gold, "and gave them presents of every sort." He housed them in the elegant and spacious palace of his father, Axayacatl, near his own residence and the great temple. Graciously he escorted them through the two lake cities; he ordered terrified servants to feed them lavishly, and see to their every need.

Once, when two Spanish sloops had been finished, Cortés delighted the emperor with a trip to a royal hunting preserve on a rocky island. There was a stiff breeze, Díaz recalled, and the sailors were delighted to please Moctezuma; "the sloop went scudding along," leaving the Aztec canoes far behind. The emperor "was charmed and said it was a great art to combine sails and oars together." He returned "very contented."

Yet he eyed the strangers with a mixture of awe and mysticism—and as the weeks passed, with rising antagonism. Exchanges of courtesy foundered on the issue of religion. Mexica envoys had offered the newly-arrived deities food soaked with human blood—and witnessed their revulsion. In the great temples the Spaniards found abominations.

As Peter Martyr recorded, they "perceived by the light of torches that the walls were stained red; and wishing to convince themselves they scratched the wall with their daggers. O horrors! not only were the walls sprinkled with the blood of human victims, but there were pools of blood two fingers deep on the floors. . . . Where the wall had been scratched . . . an intolerable odour exhaled from the decomposed blood covered with fresh blood."

*O*n one visit to the temple of Huitzilopochtli, Cortés told the priests, "It will give me great pleasure to fight for my God against your gods, who are a mere nothing." They had warned that the Aztecs were ready to die for their gods, and added insults to the Virgin. Cortés caught up an iron bar. Andrés de Tapia recalled on his faith as a gentleman that Cortés made a leap of supernatural height to smash the gold masks of the idol, crying, "Something must we venture for the Lord."

Sovereign Splendor

Turquoise mosaic gleams in a ritual mask, an attribute of such great deities as the water goddess, the fire god, and Quetzalcoatl. A "serpent mask" of precious turquoise figured in the regalia of Quetzalcoatl that Moctezuma sent to Cortés; like a god, the emperor himself wore a turquoise diadem.

Repeatedly the Spaniards had been warned, said Díaz, that Huitzilopochtli told Moctezuma to trap the invaders in the city and kill them. Cortés had struck first, within a week. He had caught the emperor off guard, seized him, and confined him in the Spanish quarters. Now he demanded that human sacrifice be stopped. Moctezuma refused. He and the Mexica would not desert their gods.

Cortés asked that a shrine to the Virgin be placed in the temple of Huitzilopochtli. Reluctantly, Moctezuma agreed to let the two images share the temple—but, he proclaimed, the Aztec gods were so displeased they wished to leave. A procession of priests bearing the images filed sadly out of the city. As if to validate the king-priest's declaration, drought struck the valley.

During the winter of 1519-1520, Moctezuma hoped for some peaceful outcome. He promised to do homage to *el Emperador* Carlos V, and handed over an astounding treasure of gold. Cortés set aside the most beautifully wrought pieces for Carlos V and melted the rest into bullion.

Then he hurried to the coast to battle a Spanish force sent to strip him of power—like Moctezuma, he was menaced by intrigue. He left fewer than 150 Spaniards in the city, all under the command of Pedro de Alvarado, a conquistador remembered as jovial, short-tempered, and cruel.

The Spaniards gave permission for the Mexica to celebrate a festival in honor of Huitzilopochtli. They fashioned a great statue of the god from amaranth-seed dough and adorned it with a rich mantle, feathers, precious stones and gold. While warriors danced and musicians performed in the temple courtyard, "when the dance was loveliest and when song was linked to song," armed Spaniards blocked all gates and passageways. As at Cholula, they feared treachery—and struck first. Sahagún probably heard from Indian eyewitnesses what followed. "They attacked the man who was drumming and cut off his arms. Then they cut off his head, and it rolled across the floor.

"They attacked all the celebrants, stabbing them, spearing them, striking them with their swords. They attacked some of

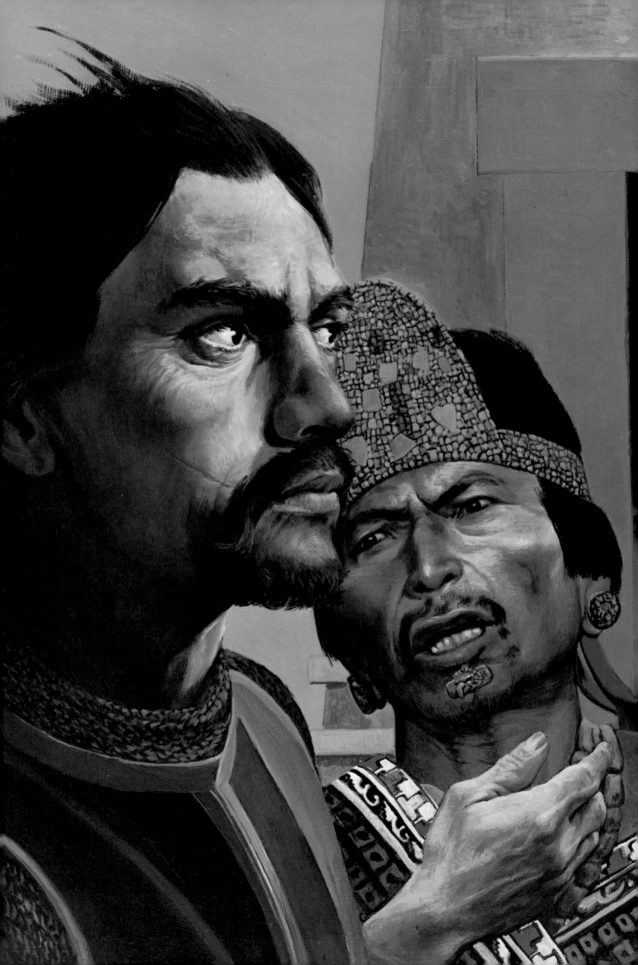

". . . if I had known that you would say such defamatory things I would not have shown you my gods; we consider them to be very good. . . ." Thus Moctezuma remonstrated with Cortés, who had called the Aztec gods "evil things." Atop the great temple of Tlatelolco, a shocked Cortés had spoken after witnessing blood-soaked shrines and burnt human hearts.

them from behind, and these fell instantly to the ground with their entrails hanging out. Others they beheaded. . . . No matter how they tried to save themselves, they could find no escape."

As the victims shrieked and wailed, warriors rushed up outside the sacred patio. "They hurled their javelins with all their strength, and the cloud of missiles spread out over the Spaniards like a yellow cloak." The Spaniards took refuge in the palace, returning fire "with their iron arrows" and their guns. "And they shackled Motecuhzoma in chains."

Cortés returned victorious, with reinforcements to a total strength of 1,300 Spaniards, to a palace besieged and a city at war. Moctezuma made a last attempt to placate his people, but they no longer obeyed. They had chosen his aggressive brother, Cuitlahuac, to replace him.

One account says that as Moctezuma addressed the Mexica from a rooftop, the young prince Cuauhtemoc, a son of Ahuitzotl, flared into anger worthy of his father. He shouted, "What is this Spaniard's wife talking about? He is a vile man and should be punished." He fired an arrow up at his cousin as others hurled a volley of stones. Moctezuma fell back, wounded in the arm, leg, and head. He lingered for a few days; then, on June 30, 1520, the emperor died. Some accounts say the Spaniards killed him, but most agree that his own subjects caused his death. Cortés is said to have wept.

On that very night, under cover of darkness and misty rain, Cortés and his troops stole out of the city. They had a portable wooden bridge to replace those removed from the causeways by the enemy. They had loaded the Spanish king's share of gold onto "seven horses, wounded and lame, and one mare and many Tlaxcatec friends, more than eighty." Soldiers grabbed up the gold bars that were left.

The armies, Spanish and Tlaxcalan, were crossing the first canal on the Tlacopan causeway when someone raised the alarm. Shouts and whistles went up in the dark, and warriors attacked along the causeway and from the lagoon. Canoes came swarming.

An Indian recalled: "The canal was soon choked with the bodies of men and horses; they filled the gap in the causeway with their own drowned bodies. Those who followed crossed to the other side by walking on the corpses." Such was *La Noche Triste*—the Night of Sorrow.

*A*t Tlacopan the Spanish toll ran to hundreds missing, all the rest wounded; and Cortés recalled, out of the twenty-odd horses that survived "not one was able to run, not a horseman able to raise an arm, not a foot soldier able to move." While the remnant hobbled toward Tlaxcala, the Mexica hunted for booty. "They gathered up everything they could find and searched the waters of the canal with the greatest care. Some of them groped with their hands and others felt about with their feet."

Harried by taunting warriors, Cortés struggled along. On an open plain near Otumba an Aztec army confronted him. Guns and powder were gone; steel remained. The war cries rang out: *"Mexico! Mexico-Tenochtitlan!" "¡Santiago—y a ellos!* Saint James—and at them!" Although suffering from a severe head wound, Cortés charged with his captains at the enemy leader, a conspicuous figure with an enormous banner of golden net. Cortés gives insight into Mexica warfare: "one of their

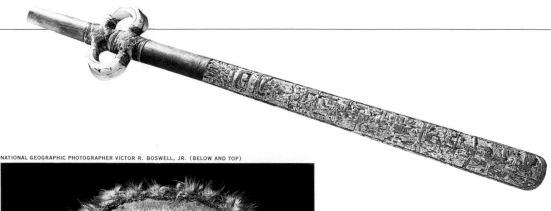

Art from a Conquest State

In a martial society, the tools of war inspired the artistry of Aztec craftsmen. A gilded atlatl, *or dart thrower (above), probably belonged to a noble warrior. The famous, time-worn sculpture at right represents one of the eagle knights. The fire-and-water symbol of sacred war streams from the mouth of a coyote on a feathered shield trimmed with gold leaf. In a desperate confrontation of well-matched valor and ill-matched weapons, Aztecs face Spaniards armed with a crossbow and harquebuses. This battle, following Moctezuma's death, nearly crushed the beleaguered Spaniards.*

army died who must have been a very important person, because with his death all that war came to an end."

While Cortés's armies recovered in Tlaxcala, death prevailed in Tenochtitlan. Spaniards left more than destruction: a plague that was probably smallpox. Sahagún's informants recalled: "we were covered with agonizing sores from head to foot. . . . A great many died from this plague, and many others died of hunger. They could not get up to search for food, and everyone else was too sick to care for them, so they starved to death in their beds." The plague claimed the new king, Cuitlahuac, after a reign of only 80 days.

In his place the Mexica elected Cuauhtemoc. His name means Descending Eagle, a symbol of the setting sun. Bernal Díaz said he was about 25, with the features and body of an aristocrat and a light complexion; not only kin to Moctezuma, he had married a daughter of the emperor, "a very beautiful woman, and young."

The young monarch prepared the Mexica to resist the Spaniards; Cortés readied his forces for invasion.

In December of 1520 Cortés secured Texcoco and used it as a base for assembling a fleet of brigantines. He reported 8,000 Tlaxcalans transporting the components as "a marvellous thing to see and, it seems to me also, to hear, this carrying of thirteen ships eighteen leagues over land." Some 20,000 warriors marched with them, eager to attack Tlaxcala's traditional enemy. From January to May Cortés was isolating Tenochtitlan. He conquered cities loyal to the Mexica, and accepted the allegiance of others. He cut off the city's supply of fresh water from Chapultepec.

Preceding pages: Under a drizzle of rain and a rain of missiles, Spanish forces make a fighting escape from Tenochtitlan on the Noche Triste—the "Night of Sorrow" in which they suffered staggering losses.

Late in April 1521, the brigantines floated onto the lagoon with flags flying and cannon firing blanks in celebration. Reinforced from the coast, the army numbered 86 horsemen, 118 crossbowmen and musketeers, and more than 700 men with sword and buckler. When the thousands of Indian allies had gathered, Cortés assigned three assault groups to Tlacopan, Coyoacan, and Iztapalapa for an attack along the causeways. These assaults met fierce resistance, but when the ships approached "the common people were terrified at the sight. They gathered their children into the canoes and fled helter-skelter across the lake, moaning with fear. . . ."

When a flotilla of armed Mexica canoes attacked, the brigantines easily dispersed it. Cannon at close range crumbled defensive walls. Street by street Spaniards moved through the city, destroying houses and filling canals with the rubble to give the horsemen access to Tenochtitlan.

As weeks passed the defenders adapted to European weaponry. "When the Aztecs discovered that the shots . . . always flew in a straight line, they no longer ran away in the line of fire. They ran to the right or left or in zigzags, not in front of the guns."

During the weeks of war the Mexica honored their gods with sacrificed captives as the Spaniards and their allies looked on in anguish. Sahagún wrote of one incident: "Some of the captives were weeping, some were keening, and others were beating their palms against their mouths. . . . One by one they were forced to climb to the temple platform. . . .

"As soon as the sacrifices were finished, the Aztecs ranged the Spaniards' heads in rows on pikes. They also lined up their horses' heads. They placed the horses' heads at the bottom and the heads of the Spaniards above, and arranged them all so that the faces were toward the sun."

Triumphant in defeat, Cuauhtemoc, last of the Aztec rulers, stands dressed in regal robes and headdress, grasping a spear. The statue of the emperor who led the last battles against the Spanish invaders surveys one of Mexico City's most important intersections. No monument in the Mexican capital memorializes Cortés.

Twice Cortés escaped death because the Mexica were intent on taking him alive for sacrifice. But sacrifice did not aid them. Fighting valiantly, they retreated to make their last stand in Tlatelolco. "Husbands searched for their wives, and fathers carried their small children on their shoulders. Tears of grief and despair streamed down their cheeks."

In desperation and faith, the Mexica resorted to their final defense. Cuauhtemoc ordered a warrior to clothe himself in ceremonial raiment that had belonged to his father, Ahuitzotl. In the warrior's hand they placed the sacred serpent-of-fire of Huitzilopochtli, the weapon the god brandished at birth to defend his mother, destroying his sister and brothers and causing them to become the moon and stars. The hero went forth to confront the enemy—"much did he terrify them, as if they had seen in him something inhuman." But no saving miracle happened. Perhaps, as Moctezuma had said, the gods had left.

Once more the enemy attacked. Flames burst from the great temple. A brigantine overtook Cuauhtemoc's canoe as he tried to escape, and the king surrendered. According to Bernal Díaz, he said to Cortés: " 'I can do no more. I have been brought before you by force as a prisoner. Take that dagger from your belt and kill me with it quickly.' Then he wept and sobbed, and the other great lords he had brought with him wept also." It was August 13.

Bodies clogged the city, said Díaz: "Even Cortés was sick from the stink in the nostrils." During the seventy-five days of the siege the Mexica had dug up roots, stripped bark from trees, for food. Cortés declared the two cities uninhabitable and ordered them abandoned.

A poet sang of the hushed ruins and the mocking god, Tezcatlipoca, The Enemy On Both Sides: "Nothing but flowers and songs of sorrow / are left in Mexico and Tlatelolco, / where once we saw warriors and wise men. . . . / Have you grown weary of your servants? / Are you angry with your servants, O Giver of Life?"

It had been nearly a century since the Mexica served as vassals to another power. Now Cortés had won their mighty empire for his own emperor. The last Mexica ruler remained a prisoner. But for Cortés, peace rankled and comfort chafed. He took Cuauhtemoc with him on a new expedition of exploration and conquest; in Yucatan, far from the borders of his former empire, Cortés accused him of treason and sentenced him to hang.

Cuauhtemoc, tradition says, died on a giant ceiba tree. An ironic end, if true, for the ceiba is the silk-cotton tree, that metaphor of greatness for the ruler, of comfort and protection for the people. When Cuauhtemoc died the Descending Eagle fell, the Setting Sun disappeared, the glorious age of the Mexica ended.

THE NATION

"The torch which is to illuminate Mexico has been lighted and today we have been given a mirror to look into."

*E*ach time I said a sad goodbye to her she gave me flowers from her garden. "If you are looking for the past," said Doña Modesta as she stopped to pick a large spotted lily, "this one to me is the most Aztec. They still grow wild here in the high forests of the volcano. And you must have one of these." She cut a rosebud. "They are my favorite."

Descending the misty slopes, I looked at the two perfect blossoms in my hand. One was a bright orange burst of petals spotted with black; the other, a pale pink bud still folded delicately upon itself. These two flowers—an Aztec, or jaguar, lily and a rose of Castile—could symbolize Mexico today.

I had expected Doña Modesta's family to preserve Indian traditions, but to my

Preceding pages: Golden haze of candlelight envelops people of Mixquic gathered for a graveside vigil on the Day of the Dead. The celebration has roots in the Great Feast of the Dead, when Aztecs honored departed souls with torch lightings and offerings to their memory.

EMBLEM, ABOVE: THE ARMS OF MEXICO, FROM THE NATIONAL FLAG

surprise she also told me a tale of the Spaniards' arrival at Hueyapan, a memory of their terrifying beasts.

"My grandmother told me, and her grandmother told her, and all the grandmothers who went before said, that when the Spaniards first came here they were riding horses. Our people had no cure for inflamed tonsils and they had never seen enormous animals like those with their big, long necks. So they asked the Spaniards for the *baba*, the foam that drips from horses' mouths after they have been running, to use as a cure. There are still people here who use horse foam for curing, but I don't. It is a juice of exhaustion. I use a kind of maguey. Juice from the earth heals."

She added this revealing comment on a mixed heritage: "Nahuatl is our language. We grow up with it. But we must learn Spanish to defend ourselves in life."

The poet Octavio Paz says of the conquest and aftermath: "If Mexico was born in the sixteenth century, we must agree that it was the child of a double violence, imperial and unifying: that of the Aztecs and that of the Spaniards."

That theme came into sharp focus for all Mexicans in March of 1981 with the improbable discovery of a relic from the Noche Triste. A workman excavating the foundation for a new building in downtown Mexico City unearthed a piece of gold weighing 4.26 pounds near the edge of a street that was once the Tlacopan causeway. The gold fashioned for an Aztec emperor had been melted to a curved form that would fit a Spanish waist. When the retreat of the Night of Sorrow became a melee for survival, the gold was hurled into the lake or fell with its desperate bearer. It sank through silt to lie on the lake bed more than 460 years while an empire fell, became a colony, grew into a nation. In presenting the new relic to the Mexican people, President José López Portillo called it "one of the great and dramatic testimonies of our national identity."

That identity is not only a mix of cultural histories but also a blend of customs and myths. Ghosts of the Aztec past still prowl. The wailing voice, an omen that came to Moctezuma II and his people, is heard to this day. *La Llorona*, the Weeping Woman, still seeks her lost children. To the Aztecs she was the mother goddess clad in white who roamed the countryside in the night crying for her lost child; the sight of her was a dreaded omen. A later tradition says she was a poor Indian who bore children to a wealthy man of Spanish descent. Abandoned and brokenhearted, she killed the children—only to repent and haunt the streets of Mexico City swathed in white. Those few who have looked upon her face have died.

In Hueyapan, Doña Modesta says, La Llorona never wanted children at all. "She got rid of them in some way, either by abortion or by killing them when they were born. Then later she was all alone. She wanders by the river, crying 'Oh, my children, my children . . .' and looking for them. Those who hear her are the women who also have caused abortions, and eventually they become Lloronas too."

At her village, adds her friend Doris Heyden, "people want and need children since it is an agricultural settlement and all hands are useful."

Often, as in Hueyapan, tales of spirits echo social concerns and serve social purposes beyond that of entertainment. Usually their origins are long forgotten. One elderly teller of tales used a metaphor

DAVID HISER

Pride, courage, and centuries of tradition inspire Totonac voladores—fliers—*to ascend to a platform 100 feet in the air. To the music of flute and drum, the four* voladores *on the platform's edge prepare to go down. Ropes tied at their ankles link them to a capstan and ensure a graceful, spiraling descent. In the ancient Aztec version of the ritual,* voladores *wore costumes representing the sacred birds of the four cardinal directions.*

Men "fallen from the sky, the stars, those sacrificed . . . to the deities of the earth," a scholar wrote of the Aztec voladores. Today at Cuetzalan in Puebla, men float earthward in an aerial paean to the Virgin. While four fliers descend, a fifth remains atop the platform—"like the sun," says a Totonac— accompanying their flight with music.

reminiscent of Tezcatlipoca when a scholar asked him about this: ". . . that is a question which even I cannot answer for I do not know. Perhaps they are of the night wind's telling."

Tezcatlipoca, Lord of the Everywhere, reminded the Mexica with the sound of his flute in the night that he knew all, saw everything in the universe. One moonless night in the darkened little schoolhouse in Xochitlan I, too, heard the eerie notes of a reed flute. They were joined by the pulsating rhythm of a drum.

A flashlight and a candle soon illuminated the dark, angular face of José García Santés, who had traveled up from coastal Veracruz with us. He was clad in the white of lowland Totonacs and he sat with his hooded eyes lowered, the small drum suspended from his little finger and his head bent to the seriousness of his music. "He is playing an invocation to the four directions," whispered Jeff Wilkerson. "They have powers. With this music he invokes their support in the ritual."

José is the most skilled of the *voladores* now practicing in Veracruz. Literally, voladores means "fliers," but the literal is the least of the matter. Their ritual—playing an invocation and then spinning head down on ropes from a high pole—is an ancient one, representing the cosmos. The four voladores suggest the four directions, and the pole represents the universal center for their spiraling revolutions downward. "A volador told me," said Jeff, " 'If done correctly it brings us closer to knowledge. In the ceremony we receive something from the supernatural and return to earth with it.' "

A quiet, peaceful man with varied roles of leadership, José trains young boys to this ritual. He begins with a low pole, and hours of patience. He speaks softly when asked if it bothers him to wring the necks of turkeys for the feasts he gives: "No. Not at all." It goes back, explains Jeff, to the ritual sacrifice of birds so common in pre-Columbian religion.

In those centuries when the gods were still young, pilgrims traveled to sacred sites to pay homage. Later, much later, some shrines became abodes of Christian saints. No one knows how long ago pilgrims began journeying to Chalma, a place of miraculous cures hidden at a rocky canyon near Malinalco, but I joined a modern pilgrimage to honor San Miguel there on his saint's day, September 29.

Traveling west and south from Mexico City, I stopped at the village of El Ahuehuete where crowds poured from buses and cars. "Our family is a sponsor of Chalma," said a young girl from the capital. "We come here every year. Our women come by bus, the men walk. On foot the journey takes about 24 hours." Many of the pilgrims walk past unmapped ancient ruins on centuries-old routes, for those who come on unshod foot to pray are considered the most meritorious.

*I*n the village, I saw first-time pilgrims don crowns of flowers and dance a shuffling two-step to the music of a violin and drum in front of an image of the Virgin of Guadalupe, patron saint of Mexico. They also danced at a sacred giant cypress, an *ahuehuete,* as in ancient times.

Vendor and visitor alike packed the slick muddy cobblestone streets of Chalma as we made our way down to the church. There we added our flowery crowns to others in an enormous growing pile, and then climbed stairs to St. Michael's cave in the cliff. Blaring bands and bursting fireworks gave the festivities a carnival air, but penitents finishing an exhausting journey on bloodied knees bespoke the seriousness of the devotions.

Inside the cave, devoted attendants brought San Miguel out of his glass case as they do annually for his day. A man from Cuernavaca had brought his church's San Miguel to share the solemn occasion.

Pilgrims' Way: Chalma and Its Holy Things

Scene of countless pilgrimages, the shrines at Chalma welcome the pious for the Feast of St. Michael, September 29. Like other Christian sites, Chalma has ties to the pagan past, when pilgrims worshiped the stone image of a deity housed in a cave nearby. According to legend, the idol was miraculously cast down and a crucifix appeared in its place. Today devotees come from throughout Mexico to pay homage at the scene of the miracle. A penitent on bended knees moves slowly toward the church; friends place cushions in her path to ease the way. A wide-eyed young visitor wears the floral crown signifying a first pilgrimage to Chalma. Entire families make the arduous trek to this canyon several miles southeast of Malinalco. Often they return home with religious objects blessed at the holy place, such as the painting of a crucifix below.

Winged and victorious,
St. Michael commands the cave at
Chalma, where an ancient idol stood. The
figure of the warrior archangel recalls
a Mexica cult long since abandoned:
that of the triumphant Huitzilopochtli.

"People once came here to an old idol," he said. "But San Miguel appeared and drove it away." The archangel as heaven's warrior wore the helmet, tunic, and armor of a Roman legionary, with a banner and a bloody sword, and stood triumphant over the devil lying vanquished at his feet.

Outside, vendors sold bars of soap at springs and where the shallow river cascaded past the church. Mothers soaped children, grown-ups scrubbed themselves. As Durán says of Aztec pilgrims: "all young and old went to bathe in the rivers to wash away the venial sins they had committed during the year. . . ." And throughout the countryside nearby I saw crosses of fresh marigolds hung over doorways and windows and on fences of pastures and fields: crosses that would keep the devil away for yet another year.

*I*n autumn, vast fields of marigolds become golden treasures offered on the Day of the Dead, November 2. Markets fill with the blossoms. Excited children in sweet shops buy sugar skulls with their names traced in icing, or a chocolate coffin with a toy skeleton inside. "The skeletons are humorous," explained my friend Maricruz Paillés, "to show death is nothing to be feared. It is another phase of our lives, nothing more."

On that day I went with Felipe Solís and Maricruz, who is also a curator at the National Museum of Anthropology, to Mixquic, once an island-chinampa town in Lake Chalco. "Mixquic was a place of contact with the Aztec underworld," Felipe said. "Today it is famous for its Day of the Dead celebration." From dusk until late that night we watched as townspeople covered relatives' graves with flowers and filled the cemetery with the smoke of candles and of burning copal incense. A platform of skulls and bones held flowers, candles, and fruit. "To honor the unknown, the forgotten ones," someone

Age-old regard for death flavors Day of the Dead observance in the town of Mixquic. Kinsmen bring candles, food, and flowers to the cemetery for the returning spirits of Little Dead Ones. Marigolds, traditional flowers of death, blanket graves and surround the skull of a nameless stranger, in remembrance of the unknown dead.

Legacy of Five Suns

Shrine to Mesoamerica's past, the National Museum of Anthropology
spans acres of parkland in Mexico City. Nearby rise the slopes of
Chapultepec, where wandering Aztecs first settled in the Valley of
Mexico. In the Museum's Mexica Hall, visitors pause before the
Stone of the Fifth Sun, a 26-ton basalt disk. Its iconography records
the Aztecs' view of the cosmos and predicts their doom with the

inevitable waning of the Fifth Sun. Aztec
pessimism fills the poetic lament carved on
a museum wall: Will I leave only this:
Like the flowers that wither?
Will nothing last in my name. . . ?
Today Aztec artistry, reflected in
the perfectly carved coils of a diorite
serpent, perpetuates their glory.

In the Mexica Hall

"Part of a distant universe of fear"— the words of anthropologist George C. Vaillant fit the colossal statue of Coatlicue. Looming over the Mexica Hall, "She of the Serpent Skirt" presents an image both horrific and profoundly compelling. Excavations

in 1790 uncovered it near the Templo Mayor; Dominicans reburied it, fearing its effect on the young. The figure sprouts a dual serpent head and wears a necklace of human hands and hearts. But such details represent Aztec concepts of procreativeness as well as death. In myth, Coatlicue held an honored place as Huitzilopochtli's mother. Perhaps more than any piece, the statue bearing her name speaks of

the power of Aztec beliefs in death as necessary for life. Head of Macuilxochitl, god of music, emerges from a tortoise shell (above). Aztec sculpture often blends earthly and divine, attesting to their belief in a dual principle which, one scholar says, "is found, like man, between sky and soil, in the mortal realm of life and death."

Images that Endure

Relic of a vanished empire, this stone jaguar held
hearts of sacrificial victims in its hollow back. From the
jaguar came ideals of strength and courage. Its
companion in the art of Tula, the coyote, appears in this
Aztec work at rest—but alert. Sacrifice and militarism
shaped and defined Aztec society, and characterized its
art. The receptacle in the jaguar's back bears carved
images of Huitzilopochtli, patron of warriors of the day,
and Tezcatlipoca, patron of warriors of the night.

said. A banner proclaimed it a *tzompantli*—the Aztec skull rack, remembered but misunderstood now. "All my grandparents are buried here," a teenager told me. "We do this each year—visit with them, remember them."

Mexico revels in remembrance of its distinguished past. I witnessed it wherever I went, with whomever I spoke. The great museum of Maricruz and Felipe welcomes millions of visitors each year, most of them Mexicans. There they view the awesome relics of Mexico's proud and turbulent past: the oldest worked stones; the little figurines from communities like Tlatilco; the splendid carvings from the Olmec sites, and the other civilizations that followed. Among the spacious chambers, the hall of the Mexica takes pride of place. In such collections Mexicans see an important part of the future. As Augusto Molina said to me, speaking of the ruined cities: "They are a cultural heritage to conserve in all their authenticity. They belong not only to us but also to the generations not yet born."

In Nezahualcoyotl's gardens at Texcotzingo, I found a youthful appreciation of that heritage. If the facts were confused, the sentiment was heartfelt. As I sat on steps leading down to the ruler's seat of stone, four young schoolboys—the oldest no more than 12—came running and laughing down the path. One boy stopped suddenly. He grew pensive. He became lost in thought as the others ran on ahead. He turned to me.

"*¡Yo soy el rey!*" he proclaimed—"I am the king!" "You?" I asked. "Yes." With conscious dignity he seated himself on the ancient throne. He leaned forward, his chin cupped in one hand, and looked out at the valley below us, the mountains around. He spread his arms wide. "I am Cuauhtemoc and these lands are mine!" he shouted. Content, he leaned back and gazed at his domain. Then he was off with a wave, running, laughing, climbing to join his companions. Ascending.

INDEX

Boldface indicates illustrations;
italic refers to picture legends.

196

Library of Congress CIP **Data**
Stuart, Gene S.
 The mighty Aztecs.

 Bibliography: p.
 Includes index.
 1. Aztecs. I. National
Geographic Society (U. S.).
Special Publications Division.
II. Title.
F1219.73.S78 972 80-8102
ISBN 0-87044-362-3 (regular binding)
ISBN 0-87044-367-4 (library binding)
        AACR2

Composition for *The Mighty Aztecs* by
National Geographic's Photographic
Services, Carl M. Shrader, Chief, Law-
rence F. Ludwig, Assistant Chief. Print-
ed and bound by Holladay-Tyler
Printing Corp., Rockville, Md. Color
separations by The Lanman Progressive
Corp., Washington, D. C.; Lincoln
Graphics, Inc., Cherry Hill, N.J.;
N.E.C., Inc., Nashville, Tenn.

*Somber splendor of the Aztec Empire
survives in this obsidian mask, possibly
made to be placed over the funerary
wrappings of the body of some
distinguished personage. Experts think
that small holes drilled in the top
permitted stitching, while larger holes
in the ears held ornaments of gold.*

Additional Reading

The reader may want to check the *National Geographic Index* for related material; the
Society has published many articles on archaeology in Mesoamerica since March
1913, with three major articles on the Aztecs in December 1980. The reader may also
consult the Special Publication *The Mysterious Maya,* by George E. and Gene S. Stuart,
and the Society's Archeological Map of Middle America.

 The standard reference is the *Handbook of Middle American Indians,* ed. Robert
Wauchope; see vols. 10, 12, 13, 14, 15, 16.

 The following may also be useful: Richard E. W. Adams, *Prehistoric Mesoamerica;*
Patricia R. Anawalt, *Indian Clothing Before Cortés;* Ignacio Bernal, *Mexico Before Cortez;*
Alfonso Caso, *The Aztecs: People of the Sun;* Michael D. Coe and Richard A. Diehl, *In the
Land of the Olmec;* Nigel Davies, *The Aztecs: A History;* Bernal Díaz del Castillo, *True
History of the Conquest of New Spain;* Fray Diego Durán, *The Aztecs: The History of the
Indies of New Spain* and *Book of the Gods and Rites and The Ancient Calendar,* tr. and ed.
Fernando Horcasitas and Doris Heyden; Patricia de Fuentes, ed. and tr., *The Conquis-
tadors: First-person accounts of the Conquest of Mexico;* Charles Gibson, *The Aztecs Under
Spanish Rule;* Doris Heyden and Paul Gendrop, *Pre-Columbian Architecture of Meso-
america;* Fernando Horcasitas, *The Aztecs Then and Now;* Benjamin Keen, *The Aztec Im-
age in Western Thought;* George Kubler, *The Art and Architecture of Ancient America;*
Miguel León-Portilla, *Aztec Thought and Culture* and *The Broken Spears;* Salvador de
Madariaga, *Hernán Cortés: Conqueror of Mexico;* René Millon, ed., *Urbanization at Teoti-
huacán, Mexico;* A. R. Pagden, tr. and ed., *Hernán Cortés: Letters from Mexico;* Esther
Pasztory, ed., *Middle Classic Mesoamerica: A.D. 400-700;* William H. Prescott, *The History
of the Conquest of Mexico;* Fray Bernardino de Sahagún, *The Florentine Codex: General
History of the Things of New Spain* and *The War of Conquest,* tr. Arthur J. O. Anderson
and Charles E. Dibble; Jacques Soustelle, *Daily Life of the Aztecs;* George C. Vaillant,
Aztecs of Mexico; Henry Raup Wagner, *The Rise of Fernando Cortés;* Muriel Porter
Weaver, *The Aztecs, Maya, and Their Predecessors;* Eric Wolf, *Sons of the Shaking Earth.*

Acknowledgments & Illustrations Credits

The Special Publications Division acknowledges with pleasure the indispensable cooperation of Mexico's Instituto Nacional de Antropología e Historia (INAH), the Museo Nacional de Antropología, the Archivo General de la Nación, and the Consejo Nacional de Turismo. The Division is equally grateful to the individuals and organizations named or quoted in the text, and to those cited here, for their generous assistance during the preparation of this book: the Academy of American Franciscan History; Dumbarton Oaks Research Library and Collections; the Smithsonian Institution; the University of Texas Press; and Patricia R. Anawalt, Pedro Armillas, Carlos Aróstegui, Pam Balough, K. Jack Bauer, Kathryn A. Bazo, Deborah A. Bell, Frances Frei Berdan, Elizabeth H. Boone, Edward E. Calnek, John Carlson, Noémi Castillo, Robin Darling, Richard A. Diehl, Theodore R. Dudley, Herbert R. Harvey, John Hobgood, Walter J. Karcheski, Jr., George Kubler, Angel Palacio B., Esther Pasztory, Victoria Velasco, Robert C. West.

The Division thanks Thelma Sullivan for permission to quote unpublished translations from Nahuatl texts (pages 32, 36, 60, 88, 89, 94-95, 124, 125, 127, 136, 137, 142, 145).

For excerpts from published material, it gratefully acknowledges the following:

Nigel Davies, *The Aztecs: A History*, copyright © 1973 by Nigel Davies. First published 1973 by Macmillan London Ltd. First published 1980 by the University of Oklahoma Press, Publishing Division of the University, Norman.

Fray Diego Durán, *Book of the Gods and Rites and The Ancient Calendar*, translated and edited by Fernando Horcasitas and Doris Heyden. Copyright 1971 by the University of Oklahoma Press, Publishing Division of the University, Norman.

Miguel León-Portilla, *Aztec Thought and Culture*, translated by Jack Emory Davis. Copyright 1963 by the University of Oklahoma Press, Publishing Division of the University.

Miguel León-Portilla, *The Broken Spears: The Aztec Account of the Conquest of Mexico*. Copyright © 1962 by Beacon Press. Excerpts reprinted by permission of Beacon Press.

Fray Diego Durán, *The Aztecs*, translated by Doris Heyden and Fernando Horcasitas. Copyright © 1964 by The Orion Press, Inc. Selections reprinted by permission of Viking Penguin Inc.

Bernal Díaz, *The Conquest of New Spain*, translated with an introduction by J. M. Cohen. Copyright © J. M. Cohen, 1963. Selections reprinted by permission of Penguin Books.

Jacques Soustelle, *Daily Life of the Aztecs on the Eve of the Spanish Conquest*. Copyright © Librairie Hachette, 1955. English translation by Patrick O'Brian. Copyright © 1961 by George Weidenfeld & Nicolson Ltd. By permission George Weidenfeld & Nicolson Ltd. and Librairie Hachette.

Quotations used as chapter headings:
P. 18: said of the Toltecs; in León-Portilla, *Aztec Thought and Culture*, p. 167. P. 36: said of the Chichimecs; in Anales de Cuauhtitlan (Códice Chimalpopoca), translated by Thelma Sullivan. P. 60: from an Aztec poem; in León-Portilla, *Aztec Thought and Culture*, p. 166. P. 94: Moctezuma II, on the death of prisoners; in Durán, *The Aztecs*, p. 246. P. 124: from the Florentine Codex, Bk. 6; translated by Thelma Sullivan. P. 152: from an Aztec "song of sorrow"; in León-Portilla, *The Broken Spears*, p. 137. P. 180: from a coronation address by Nezahualpilli; in Durán, *The Aztecs*, p. 221.

Equally, for illustrations, it thanks the following:
The Museo Nacional de Antropología: P. 1 (width, 1 m). P. 19, right (ht., 11 cm). P. 33 (ht., 73 cm). P. 54, sculpture (length 46 cm). P. 61, left (ht., 62 cm). P. 97, drum (length 60 cm). Pp. 100-01 (diameter 2.7 m). P. 118 (42 x 29 cm). P. 132 (ht., 1m, 15 cm). P. 136, left (ht., 80 cm). P. 149 (ht., 33 cm). P. 173 (ht., 32 cm). P. 191 (ht., 55 cm). P. 192, top (ht., 38 cm). Pp. 192, 193, Coatlicue (ht., 2.52 m). Pp. 194-95, jaguar

(ht., 93 cm). P. 195, coyote (ht., 38 cm). P. 198 (ht., 20 cm).

The Templo Mayor project, INAH: P. 19, left (ht., 10 cm). P. 61, right (ht., 24.5 cm). Pp. 74-75. Pp. 76-77. P. 78, left (ht., c. 15 cm), right (ht., 21.5 cm). P. 79 (ht., 20 cm). P. 80, top (ht., 34 cm); lower: left (ht., 11.9 cm), center (ht., 10.7 cm), right (ht., 9.5 cm). Pp. 80-81. P. 83, top, bottom. Pp. 84-85.

Akademische Druck-u. Verlagsanstalt, Graz, Austria: Pp. 18, 36, 60, 94, 124, 152, Aztec deities drawn from facsimile of the Codex Borbonicus. Pp. 33, 56, 89, 119, 148, 177, 195, colophon from facsimile of the Codex Magliabecchiano.

The collection of Dr. George E. Stuart: P. 50, from the Florentine Codex, facsimile by Archivo General de la Nación (original: Biblioteca Medicea Laurenziana, Florence, Italy). P. 130, p. 139, from the Codex Mendoza in Lord Kingsborough's *Antiquities of Mexico*, 1829.

Dumbarton Oaks, Pre-Columbian Collection: P. 6, from the Lienzo de Tlaxcalla, plate 2 in Alfredo Chavero, *Antigüedades mexicanas . . .*, 1892. P. 146, from the Florentine Codex, facsimile by Archivo General. P. 163, from the Lienzo de Tlaxcalla, plate 45 in Chavero.

Cartón y Papel de México, S.A.: Pp. 153 (both), 172 (bottom), from facsimile, *Los Tlacuilos de Fray Diego Durán*.

The Bodleian Library, Oxford, England: P. 64, folio 2, Codex Mendoza. P. 144, folio 65, Codex Mendoza.

The Museo Preistorico ed Etnografico Luigi Pigorini, Rome, Italy: P. 169 (ht., 24 cm). P. 172, *atlatl* (length, 56 cm). The Bibliothèque Nationale, Paris, France: P. 43, from Historia Tolteca-Chichimeca; drawn after facsimile ed. Paul Kirchhoff et al., INAH, 1976. The Museum für Völkerkunde, Vienna, Austria: P. 172, shield (diameter, 69 cm). The Museum of Mankind, London, England: Pp. 146-47, knife (overall length, 33.75 cm). The Museum für Völkerkunde, Staatliche Museen Preussischer Kulturbesitz, Berlin, West Germany: P. 112. (ht., 60 cm).

To convey the freshness of originals now time-worn, Mark Seidler of the Society's staff drew and colored the artwork on pp. 18, 36, 43, 60, 94, 124, 152, and 180.

Artifacts not otherwise credited were photographed by: David Hiser: Pp. 61 left, 78 left, 79, 91, 97, 100-01, 118, 195. NGS Photographer Victor R. Boswell, Jr.: Pp. 54, 112, 136 left, 146-47, 169, 191 lower, 194-95. C. E. Petrone, NGS Staff: Pp. 6, 146, 163. Melinda Berge: Pp. 19 left, 61 right, 78 right.

A Note on the Aztec Language

Nobody knows precisely how the Aztecs pronounced their language, classical Nahuatl, because it was written down after 1521 following Spanish rules for Spanish sounds. Modern pronunciation is easier than it looks.

Vowel sounds are, roughly, ah (as in father), ay (as in day), ee (as in meek), oh (as in toe). Before a and o the consonant **c** is rather like our *k*; so is **qu** before *e* or *i*. **Cu** before vowels is pronounced kw (almost as in quit), and **ch** as in church. An **hu** stands for *w* (as in we), and **tz** for the *ts* sound in cats. Before e and i, a c has the s sound in so or kiss, as does every **z**. The **x** is always like *sh* in she.

Some examples: Mexica—may-SHEE-kah; Huitzilopochtli—weets-eel-oh-pohch-tlee; and Tenochtitlan—tay-nohch-TEE-tlahn.

Stress usually falls on the next-to-last syllable. Because in some cases this differs from Spanish usage, Spanish-speaking writers add accents on Nahuatl words. Following the practice of most scholars in this country, this book does not use accents except in direct quotations. In quotations, some variant spellings appear.

Spanish usage has altered some Nahuatl place-names. Thus Cuauhnahuac (Near the Trees) has become Cuernavaca (Cow's Horn); the suffix **-tzinco,** meaning "honored place," has become *-cingo*. Other suffixes of place-names are **-can, -nahuac** (near), **-pan** (on), **-tlah** and **-tzalan** (among), and, of course, **-co,** as in Mexico.

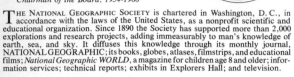